M000021343

Hybrid Vigor

A True Reveal of Love

Transcendent
Publishing

teZa Lord

Hybrid Vigor
A True Reveal of Love
By teZa Lord

Copyright © 2019 teZa Lord

All rights reserved.

Transcendent Publishing
PO Box 66202
St. Pete Beach, FL 33736
www.transcendentpublishing.com

Transcendent
——Publishing——

Cover art by teZa Lord
Illustrations by teZa Lord

ISBN-13: 978-0-9600501-8-5

Library of Congress Control Number: 2019905628

Printed in the United States of America.

for Eve Mary, who taught me how to Be Love

CONTENTS

PART ONE: I WALK IN LOVE vii

meeting new lovers … just about anywhere............................ 1

love junkie 11

pagan mama.. 23

the unlikely web of love you, hate you................................. 31

we are one 39

we are but guests of nature 49

suspended in expectation 67

the alchemy of love... 73

my two mothers 93

the messiness of loving... 105

amazed and astounded 117

being a hybrid vigor.. 127

who are we, really?... 139

sinners and saints, skunks and stingrays.............................. 155

PART TWO: BECOMING A HYBRID VIGOR.................. 167

creatively conscious.. 169

healing using energy 187

#UsToo 195

a love worth living for 203

shit happens – so hold on! 213

the party (and religion) of love 225

the ecstasy of love-onomics.. 239

being … one.. 245

ABOUT THE AUTHOR.. 251

PART ONE

i walk in love

the time of the power wave dream ... is here

CHAPTER 1

meeting new lovers …
just about anywhere

The distant call had sounded many times but I couldn't have known its meaning, not then. Whenever the feral rooster's musical croaking alarm woke me up—it was as if hearing his crow through cotton wads stuffed in my ears, so accustomed was I to not seeing, hearing, sensing in any way, anything other than my own get-even fight against life.

Until that day when I finally understood Roostie's far-off cry, I couldn't have known that the time of that power-wave dream, the one that lifted me sky high, so I could see forever, forewarning me about these times, now … was here at last.

I'd come to the end of a real-life love, but not what you'd call an affair of the heart. *Loving* another was more an obsession than an enjoyment for me. The habit of "Being in Love"—the method I chose to rise above red-hot anger or scared-stiff insecurity that otherwise consumed me if I wasn't actively engrossed with another person's life—caused me to be immune to the delayed state of Self-knowing that others so easily seemed to imbibe in. I wish it weren't so. I wish freedom from obsessing had happened to me earlier, and easier. The capriciousness of others' and my own untrustworthiness, fueled by my paralyzing sense of deep distrust—which only later I came to identify as self-loathing—was what pushed me into believing, naively, that the thrill of *being in love* was the only reasonable antidote to my personal misery.

My first childhood loves were trusting bumblebees in my mom's kitchen garden, then the hilariously humorous chickens roosting in the "fowl house," and the amusingly intelligent pigs, all of whom were my chores to tend whenever I stayed, weeks at a time, at my grandparents' New Jersey farm.

I got along better with animals than other kids, other people. Whether pet dogs, cats, rabbits, or white mice I raised for 4-H projects, back in my rural upbringing, I loved them all. I could trust the rare sight of a doe as it crept closer to my silent form, crouched in a still meadow, a heart-stopping momentous event, the way I figured real love ought to be. One summer, as a teen, I was courted by a persistent swallow, who would alight on top of my head, day after day, as I sat in a field, my head dwarfed by the umbrella blooms of Queen Anne's lace, writing in my always-nearby secret journal.

Ahh, I thought, feeling tiny pricks of the bird's feet upon my scalp, *This is how real lovers are meant to be. Amusing, unpredictably entertaining, and always, always as trusting and fond of me as I am of them.*

Yet I wasn't to find a human love who had such flair or favor as my animal companions, in the human slush pile I was to go through.

I didn't know I could trust another person, let alone my own self. Everything I thought, said, or did as a still-asleep version of myself, I doubted. Still, when Roostie crowed, I heard, not yet knowing what he was crowing about.

Later, starting with Bruce, then Tim, breaking up was always the inevitable end of a self-fulfilling legacy. *No love is good enough, compared to how I feel about animals.*

Who could measure up to the wiles of an animal, domestic or wild? Most humans have forgotten they themselves *are* animals, let alone allow themselves to act freely from the purely inbred instincts of our more naturalism-oriented, primitive forebears. The primordial ooze from where higher life forms, microorganisms, or animals, such as you and I have all evolved, is a good part of the common denominator of all that currently exists on Earth.

I'm ready to give up on love, I screamed inside. *I've come to a dead-end.*

I came to this point, grumbling and disgruntled, after too many years of the same love-sick acting-out foolishness of mine. Explaining it to a friend once, I said, "One turned out to be gay. Another tried to drown me. Still another pressed his fingerprints into my bare arms when I tried to leave the S.O.B."

I didn't think one person could ever fill the shoes of the type of love I was looking for, one that satisfied me to utter completion. The kind I felt most comfortable dancing next to—the devil-may-care kind that died out with Billy the Kid, Annie Oakley, Wyatt Earp. Even out West, where I went a-lookin', and did my share of desert-grown peyote while I was at it—never produced my fancy's fill there either. Whatever relationship I was in, would start off hot but always ended with a puddle of frigid ice water once I realized another human could never come close to that kind of love I was looking for.

Why, you may ask, was it so important anyway, to love? Was it so I could feel more alive, more human? I didn't know the answer to that either. All I knew was I had this compulsion of needing to love, to feel alive. As if I had to conquer love. I'd repeatedly have to find it, use it, realize its deficiencies, then throw it away.

Sad, I know. But this is who I was. A love addict.

I continued searching, pushing my will, my desire, my lust to connect with some one other. Until I realized other life sources besides my human one might satiate my desires. I pushed my resources to the limits, in my wildly diverse search for the perfect lover. From the biting cold of Massachusetts winters to the warm balmy breezes of the West Indian tropics—I discovered the thrill of sailing on the deep blue sea. The great love of my life—the Ocean! At last!

Then, the Pacific. I was delighted to awake one morning with a huge humpback whale courting the underbelly of the small ketch I was on, as we flopped about in the doldrums off the coast of Nicaragua. Nobody wanted to use up the gas, so the four of us onboard drifted all day with no wind until nightfall. The boat I was crewing on was a hundred miles offshore, trying to bypass the piratical Sandinistas of the 70s who would stop any private boat that was heading for the Panama Canal, hoping to hostage the crew for a hefty ransom. That's why we sailed so far from land, to avoid that scenario.

The three others and I languidly watched the back and forth patient courtship dance of our boat's many-ton suitor, hoping to arouse the wooden lover he'd found. His efforts went on for the entire day. Only when the sun went down and the winds picked up could the sailboat make enough headway to tear away from the embrace of its cetacean lover. I was fascinated.

Quietly I followed my animal lover's gentle beckoning. I wondered, *Is it the cute protruding belly of this wooden ketch that turns him on; or could it be me, watching his obsessive dance with our vessel?*

The whale never touched our boat, was never a threat. But the gentle, massive leviathan was a Supreme Sensation to behold. I was tempted to jump overboard and mount my too-far distant teasing lover's neck, but … he didn't have one.

Once, on the shore of Florida, equipped with a trusty neoprene wetsuit one cold winter day, I slowly entered the frigid Gulf waters off Siesta Key, in Sarasota. In a short while I saw the familiar, fleeting dark streak of a dolphin's jump.

I thought to myself, *Now's as good a chance as I'll ever have, to prove how far I'm willing to go, to check out these desires I have, to know wild animals better. So much has been made about us humans communicating with all species; from bygone days' benign flea circuses to ferocious Vegas lion acts, training creatures to suit our will, entertaining others with animals' forced captivity.*

I treaded the chilly water. *I'm going to see if I can call these wild critters to me using only my thoughts.*

I didn't want to train anything. I just wanted to share my lust of life with a porpoise at that moment, if I could. With this sole, spontaneous thought, I swam gently toward the dark slice of fin I'd just spied. Deciding to test my subtle abilities I kept my head above water, so I could see three-hundred-and-sixty-five degrees around me.

Much has been speculated about interspecies communication. This curiosity of mine didn't arise from wanting to be a behavioral scientist like John Lily, or to make love with another species, Catherine the Great-style—oh no. My desires were fueled by wanting to feel more alive, to feel the fulfillment of locking eyes, raising voices together with another species. To imbibe in the intimacy that communing life forms can emote—sharing, caring, and yes, daring to know something so different, so intimately embracing ... as an encounter with another animal in the wild.

Bees, great blue herons, and dolphins have always felt like ultra-conscious cousins to me, more than other species we humans share this floating blue ball in space with.

I swam right toward where I'd spied the dorsal fin silently slice the glassy sea. I quieted my mind, and silently spoke, *Come. You can trust me.*

Slowly frog-kicking, my head rotating to scan the horizon in all directions—I then saw another dark fin! Its shininess arced above the water, for just a moment. Not a joyful jump but a low eyeball rumble. *Was it the same fellow? A scout?* I wondered. This jump was further away, so I slowly headed in that next direction, my neck extended high, focused on that new spot, yet scanning the horizon from both corners of my eyes. Absolutely riveted on thinking, *Come, my friend!* I silently beckoned them.

My mind, made still. My thoughts, now focused on only wanting to meet some new watery friends. A bit further away, behind me now, I saw another split tail break the still waters on that no-surf day in the Gulf of Mexico. Breast-stroking with head up, I swam gently toward this other direction. For the next space of time I zig-zagged my way, following the here-and-there jumps that were becoming steadier, yet always at a distance.

Silently I kept calling *Come!* a simple unspoken sound sent as a beacon, inviting them to be with me by thought alone. My intention was Love. My mental signal, an invitation to come know my Love, if you can imagine something like this for a moment. My entire being became … Love inviting Love.

Suddenly they were here! In one terrific moment an entire pod came zooming close to me, appearing in a split second from nothingness, coming from all directions! To check me out, I guessed, marveling how the creatures had heard me, responding to my silent call. There were so many, what to do? I wanted to feel them, without making swimming part of my effort. Quickly I decided to head to the sandbar I knew was close by. As I stroked, with my head high, I could see many large sleek bodies create surface wavelets from their enthused motion. I reached the sandbar that was some distance off Siesta Key beach. I'd come here often, searching for sand dollars, standing in waist-high water, using my wiggling toes to find the embedded hard-shelled creatures right below the sea floor's sandy surface.

I now stood at my full height, suddenly in the middle of this pod of magnificent cetacean beings who jubilantly surrounded me with their watery antics, there on the sandbar. I was inwardly moved, occupied by Bliss and Joy and Thrill. Too busy to realize how I'd come to be here; definitely the only one of my kind among this exuberant crowd of *others*.

And then, the fun began.

Not wanting to seem intrusive or frighten them, or give any misleading cues besides wanting to share mutual passions, I proceeded to make myself as non-threatening as possible to my new friends. Instead of those who seek the next thrill on life's endless smorgasbord, like swimming with wild dolphins—joining them in their own turf in deep coastal waters, in the Florida Keys or Hawaiian Islands or other tropical places—I didn't want to intrude on my friends' space. I remained standing tall in the waist-high water now, in the shallows of the sandbar to which I'd swum.

All around me the dolphins jumped, wrestled, tumbled, laughing with clicks and whistles like giddy teens with their long-toothed mouths opened wide as they spun by, upside down, coming within an arm's length but never touching me. I felt each animal's energy as it sped by. By some invisible protection, a safe distance remained between us. They never touched me, nor I, them. Regardless, I felt compelled to join in their antics from this vantage point of mine, standing on the sandbar, once I saw there was no danger. Their teeth looked very large and very pointy. Their bodies were more enormous, more aggressive than I at first was comfortable with. But I grew accustomed to their boisterousness.

Unconsciously, I began to sing a high-pitched sound—an animal-like monotone *babee-babee-babee*—and started swishing the water with my hands ... to feel more part of the fun, I guessed, not doubting my instincts in this hypnotic scenario unfolding before my eyes. Their hefty bodies surprised me, up close. Each animal, a different hue, a different size, rising up out of the crests of small waves the pod's antics made, creating a crazy surf that broke onto the shallow sandbar. They stuck their gleaming gray and darker heads out of the water, laughing as they looked at me, as curious, as intrigued as I was.

Then—they grew more wild with their games. Two and three dolphins wrestling in a locked fin-grip as they sped directly around me playing noisy games, singing, chortling ... and then ... they grew even more rambunctious as I continued swishing the chilly winter sea with my hands, calling that strange *babee-babee* song that came out of me, standing otherwise perfectly still in one place. Some of the wrestling beasts rushed right by me, coming ever closer with each new pass. Other pairs and trios rolled by together, looking up at my eyes as they swam on their backs, laughing with and at me. Some hugged each other in carefree coupling, their gleaming genitals as exposed as their trust of my human presence, as they went about their games, allowing me to feel truly a part of their pod.

The carnival went on for some time. I don't know how long. I was completely enchanted as I stood swishing water, calling my *babee-babee* song, watching, happy to be accepted by them but not wanting them to get any closer. With those long and sharp big white teeth! And their bodies were *way* larger, *much* stronger up close like this, than whenever I'd seen them from above the water, on the deck of a boat, or in those sad, but I knew, necessary-for-studying, salt water aquariums.

Only because the cold was now starting to bite through my wetsuit did I finally awake from my reverie … and realized I had to go.

I had no idea how much time had elapsed. Time no longer existed. Only cold now did.

The chilly water's pierce had become unbearable. My wetsuit no longer protected me. Regrettably, I had to bid farewell to my exuberant friends of an-altogether-different species, and forced myself out of my trance to turn toward the beach. But—what I saw was almost as much of a jolt as my new aquatic friends had delivered. There, on the beach, I saw only a rude interruption to my delightful play with pure Love.

Behind my back on that winter's day beach, hundreds of people had gathered on the shoreline to watch this incredible sight—me and my dolphin lovers. Eerily, the human silhouettes stood, every one of them in startled awed silence.

I instantly figured, *They've become transfixed by this playful interlude of ours, two different life-forms meeting in sheer fun, with no agendas. Or maybe they think me one hell of a wild animal trainer.* I chuckled at that notion.

I turned back to my porpoise friends. *I'm not ready to leave you, ever! The crowds, the questions, the intrusions*, I couldn't bear the thought. I shuddered, and not just from the cold water. The wars, arguments, complaints. The endless opinions, rudeness and other harsh realities of modern life all flooded my mind in one instantaneous, cruel tsunami of aversion and disgust. I turned back toward them, my true lovers, wanting to ask the dolphins if I could go with them when they returned to the open sea. But then I remembered who I was. *What* I was.

I didn't want to turn facing the beach and see these strangers of my own kind. But the cold seared through the wetsuit now. With my eyes fixed on them I slowly walked backwards toward the beach, determined to prolong my joyous contact, using my mental link and that infantile *babee-babee* song of mine to stay connected with my porpoise loves for as long as I could. Only when I reached the shallows, and the water came up to my mid-calf, did the pod of thirty or so individuals slowly disperse, a few at a time. Until two stragglers, then one, and then ... none were left, just as the fine-grained sandy shore met my cold bare feet.

I breathed deeply, needing courage before turning around. And, for the last time, I watched the still water into which my friends had quietly disappeared, just as quickly as they'd arrived an eternity ago. Not a single dark fin broke the glassiness of my scanning. Only after checking did I turn and agree to return to my own challenging, often confusing, word-based world of too many differences and not enough love.

I managed to slip silently past the large crowd, keeping my eyes focused on the sand, riveted on each next footstep ahead of me. When some woman, ostentatiously dressed with a huge turquoise floppy hat rushed up to me, to ask in an entitled, intrusive manner ... "How did you ...?"

For a split second I glanced directly into her eyes, muttering, "I can't speak now."

... occupied by bliss, joy, and thrill ...

CHAPTER 2

love junkie

The sound of Roostie's crowing draws nearer, making me smile. Nothing can stop this animal from doing its thing, not the weather, fear of intimacy, or any roaming predators out to eat his shiny red-feathered ass at their earliest convenience. Each day Roostie, with a glad heart, does his thing. Against all odds, he makes everyone who hears him loosen up, smile, and … pay attention.

A new day is upon us, that's what Roostie is crowing about, loudly, clearly.

What can I say, I'm a bona-fide love nut. My parents told me, "Sure, you're a love child! You'd fall over backwards as an infant, just laughing away."

It's true, I was born of two who loved each other very dearly. Love is that powerful an energy that it jumps from lovers right into the very soul of the seed they've planted together, in the mingling of their sacred love ritual. Yet even a child born from an unwanted rape is still a child of love, as all infants are pure and whole when they come into this world, regardless of their parentage.

Destined to explore love the way others become obsessed with exploring the poles, or testing death with their extreme challenges—there's no other way to describe the insatiable yearning to know love that I've had since childhood, other than to say it's my life calling. Obsession sounds too commonplace. To climb Love's Everest, to dive its deepest oceanic depths of human emotions, crossing each and every great plain and desert horizon and sea trench, sledding the frozen crevassed tundra, to dance with abandon what exploring Love has put in front of me—this has been my heart's desire, my lifelong quest.

I have no qualms in calling myself a love junkie. This itch to feel my heart blaze in fiery adoration, sparking from all directions, proud to have what others are embarrassed and blush at: an addiction to love. All my life I've seen eyes roll, heard the guffaws, noticed brows raised in astonishment when someone observes my persistent need for a love fix—to this very day.

Today I can laugh along with others, how ridiculous I must seem. But instead of willy nilly loving all over the place, today I proclaim myself a well-focused lieutenant in the Army of Love. Gladly, and every day, I do battle with the myriad enemies of Love, taking as many hostages as possible in my drive to encourage others to join me.

It all started when, as a youngster, I fell in love with Nature with a capital "N."

Before I could read or write I proclaimed all in the natural world as my lovers, all mine!

Each drop of dew, each clap of thunder, each buzzing bee I held in my little paws was coveted, as I felt its energy enter me, penetrating the deepest regions of my expectant heart that drummed with excitement—over more joy awaiting me—everywhere! All I had to do … was find it.

Then … adolescence, when childhood's utopia crumples. Implacable, immutable, universal Love was replaced with yukky shame and blame, put on by the inescapably puny human condition called *growing up*. Really, it should be called growing *down*, too many of us fall from grace by growing up. Regrettably, I feared I'd never fly like an angel, even if I wished to learn how, like I did so easily, so naturally in my dreams.

Belief in things *magical*—my synonym for loving dirt, trees, rocks, water, clouds, fire, hugging frogs, twirling in an open field under hurling strikes of a summer afternoon's lightning storm—was soon relegated to the fears in which others taught me to store such fantasies. By my teens I'd been called, perhaps blessedly, as all artists have to get used to it, deemed as we are by most of society to being, a tad *loony*.

The magnificence of the entire universe I claimed mine, all and everything, Nature enveloped me. I became each thunderclap, twirled myself into joining with each lightning bolt flung to earth. By age five I was as comfortable with the marvels as well as the mishaps of Nature, as old-marrieds are at accepting each other's eccentricities. Right up close to Nature's face, in *It* even, I felt the whispering of comfort that I wasn't alone. Patiently, I explored each and every particle, blade of grass, vein on a plant, as preciously as a temple girl gathers blossoms to make a beautiful garland to adorn the revered deity on the dais inside.

After puberty, I started exploring others besides my cosmic love of all things natural. I wore each conquered heart around my neck like an inadvertent Aphrodite, a bleeding-mouthed Kali mourning the end of her true love, Nature *It-self*, because I'd been rudely ripped away from Her. By my early twenties, along with my own inner pain, I clearly realized the pain Nature Herself was experiencing from manmade interference and indifference. The environmental crisis shouted "STOP!" to my ever again regarding myself a lover of Nature, if I continued sitting back, simply enjoying myself. No! There was too much work to do. I had to help, didn't I? Isn't this the true sign of a person who loves—they care for what they adore, often more than for themself? Unconditionally. So, I determined to reach out to help the object of my adoration.

I got distracted, though. First, by a shaggy-haired poet who introduced me to not only pleasures of the corporeal body but also to the delight of the sharpened, precise aesthetics of words we use to paint images. Original ideas, stories, word-thoughts now became alive, through works of art I was creating myself. From memories of the innumerable gifts my beloved Nature had so graciously bestowed upon me: I drew, painted, praised with a few chosen words, our connection, our Oneness. Creativity became the heart-connection between myself and what I once had, but sadly, had now lost: pure Oneness with Nature. With creative abandon, I threw myself into loving others as well as making art meant to re-create Nature's transcendent glory.

Alas, the poet was cast aside when he too, proved too human, too flawed.

Then came the sculptor, whose handling of hard stone stirred dust in my heart chambers as much as grit from his studio-chiseling found its way into every nook and cranny of our artist loft.

A modern-day pirate came next, providing some of the familiar thrills that Nature once had tossed my way: unexpected events, madly-daring deviltry, constant changes. Together, the Caribbean based ex-pat and I explored our mutual need to live off the grid, to be self-sufficient. One swarthy rogue was replaced by another as I took to the sea like a baby whale to its mother's doorknob-sized nipple. Until the storms of life—and those damn West Indian hurricanes—hit full force to awaken me from my rummy reverie, a newly acquired habit that went along with the buccaneer bad boys I was hanging with.

Off to the Middle East went I, this time with a lanky, sporty lover-boy who promised familial care as well as exotic adventure. He provided a warm-blooded nest in which I could start feeling, maybe trust others again. There, in Hawkeye's embrace, I crossed over from years of searching for love, to the other side of being inundated by the full force of its demands. When the Hawk and I married on a small West Indian island, before boarding a plane for

Israel, his home, my demeaning addictions had multiplied again, to match his. By marrying a boozehound, pothead and coke freak, I transitioned from a *love* junkie to a *plain ol'* one. My new and fickle lover became self-destruction.

Living a full year in a suburb of Tel Aviv as a *Shiksa*, a non-Jewish woman, I indulged in a life of wants and their accompanying disappointments. I wanted to share my quests for love's completion in paint, in words, and any other medium I could get my hands on. Adding onto the extremely tense circumstances of living in the constant war-like Holy Land, its citizens nearly as conflicted and anxious as I, being surrounded by Arab nations wishing Hawkeye and his Israelite clan, gone—I drank, smoked, and snorted more than my share. Tension and angst fluttered my heart; bad formaldehyde-laced wine poisoned my body's every cell during this sad attempt at seeking a mirage-like love-fix via a loveless marriage.

Transporting ourselves when Hawkeye's work contract was up, we fled to New York City, where my passion for passion got peeled to its core, baked to perfection, as everyone knows: the Big Apple works its caramelizing intensity on those who venture there unsteadily or unfocused.

Divorce number two. I didn't mention divorce number one because that was an error, a fluke of my insouciant kindness. Years before Hawkeye, I'd offered to marry a friend of mine for his U.S. citizenship; so that marriage really doesn't count. A vow made out of kindness is a fake promise. My irreverence for the institution of marriage was so notable back then, I married this friend, also an Israeli, in spite of the supposed sanctity of that ritual. Only to have that too, backfire on me when he—foolishly devoid, just as I was, of any knowledge of real love, other than nationalistic, thanks to the kibbutz this Israel-born man was raised on, where children are too early removed from their biological parents—he mistakenly thought he fell hard for his sacrificing friend, me. So again, I had to flee.

After splitting from Hawkeye in New York City, more screwed up than ever but at least free of my druggy, rich enabler, a random coin-toss of fate landed me chasing yet another of love's shiny red-bottomed baboons. This time in a not-so-merry spree that began in lower Manhattan and ended (some say inevitably) in a raunchy jail cell in the netherworld of the Dominican Republic's dangerous borderland with Haiti.

Where, for a crime I hadn't committed, I was thrown into a cesspool of a cell without a trial, in a place called *la fortaleza*, the local military, police station, prison combined-complex. Whose foreign name would make a mighty fine heehaw affront years later—an entire lifetime afterwards—when I sat at an elegant celebration table where one of the other couples, affluent up the Cartier kazoo, were bragging about "The splendid accommodations we had at our last resort in the D.R., the Dominican Republic." Hopelessly irreverent, I couldn't help myself. This was a target of unabashed materialism too good to miss. When the bejeweled wife asked others at dinner if they enjoyed that tropical country as much as she and her husband had, I answered, "Why yes. I had a lovely stay at one of D.R.'s finest … La Fortaleza."

Decades before that dinner party, after leaving Hawkeye and the Big Apple, I'd been mistakenly imprisoned there, with an ex-boyfriend in the next cell, whom I'd been visiting to help organize an agricultural export-business based from Santo Domingo. While Solstice languished in the crowded concrete cell adjacent to mine, I suffered immeasurably—innocent for probably the first time in my thirty-some years of misadventuring. In jail, whether innocent or not, one is forced to take a good long look at what, precisely, in your life *got you there*. What I saw wasn't pretty. But it was factual. Invisibly written upon my bare cell's ugly walls for me alone to see, loud and clear. I hated to admit it, but I desperately needed to have been caught and thrown into that damn jail.

Three months later, I was finally freed, saved by my rescuer. Not the American Embassy, which had declared a hands-off policy on this politically embarrassing affair of mine, the details of which are as intricate, as insane as the list of nameless lovers I leave unmentioned here. Notably, the lovely botanist who, many years after we broke up, would die too young, so tragically, of AIDS. I apparently, being the only person in the whole wide world who never suspected he was obviously gay; "coming out" a reference only to debutantes at that backwards time. No, my rescuer from that D.R. jail cell was the first, the strongest male lover of any girl's life. The one who tried, but failed to have taught me how to love more properly.

My father.

Dad pulled off a miracle and got me out of that hell-pit prison, just by showing up in Barahona, a cursed *pueblo* in the D.R. where I was held, close to the Haitian border. The mere presence of Dad's big tall macho gringo-ness was enough to intimidate any self-respecting Latino. Dad strongly impressed the trial judge who wore, along with ceremonial black robes, a ridiculous black beanie topped by an incongruous baby-blue pompom. Every day of the weeks-long trial, the same judge peered out from behind a forbiddingly sanctimonious wooden crucifix, fixed altar-like upon the high, stifling hot courtroom dais.

After my acquittal, Dad and I flew back to the States together. At the tail end of our journey to my parents' home-sweet-home, my father shared with me, his youngest daughter—a grown woman fresh out of a third world prison—the story he'd never told anyone before. Staring at the heart-piercingly gorgeous, lightning-sparked, blue-black crimson-streaked sky, as our tiny chartered plane's pilot, his ears thankfully covered with a headset radio, arced us over the Florida horizon on our long journey's last leg home, I listened to what my self-blaming dad asked me to listen to, uninterruptedly.

"Bad things happened to me when I was a boy," my dad named Linwood said. "Between seven and fourteen, repeatedly." He took a big gulp of the plane cabin's stale air before saying next, "I was repeatedly raped by a trusted Scoutmaster whom my parents unwittingly allowed too close to our family.

"That's why"—Dad was speaking just loud enough to be heard above the engine's roar, looking sadder than I've ever seen him as he gazed out from the plane's windshield at the many faraway electrical storms scattered on that evening's vast background, eerily lighting up the state's flat, steamy land with pastel fireworks illuminating the inky blackness during that unforgettable night's flight— "I've not been a very good father to you and your sister. I'm sorry. I just couldn't be there for you, sweetheart. Before now."

Everything erupted inside me that very instant.

Hearing my father apologize for having giving me such love, so wholeheartedly when I was a child, then breaking that bond of trust as soon I grew to be an adolescent pest, being nothing to him but challenging, a mischievous daredevil, I admit—my heart cracked open. The love I'd stored in there for my own innocent self, long forgotten, along with the bees and black-eyed does, long lost in yesterdays, now spilled out onto my lap.

Both my father's and my tears wet the spot where our locked-away fears landed before us: naked, out in the open for the first time. The charter pilot's bulky headphones kept him unaware of our conversation. Hearing my rescuer explain his own pain, hearing Dad ask my forgiveness for having broken the childhood faith I'd put in him, in love, in life itself—I melted. Even though I couldn't bring myself to speak to him of the terrible abuse I'd suffered from another family member—not yet, not then—I felt empowered by my father's opening up to me about the pain he admitted carrying all his life.

That's when I let Self Love, feeling Spirit *living within*, as part of me, begin to heal me. Not the shrink-wrapped variety, not the fake kind; not the get-laid and get-gone kind, either. This is when I felt a great shift inside me. This is when I began to *want to be* ... a *hybrid vigor*.

Hearing Dad speak about his long-held secret pain, released me from my self-imposed prison of not believing in any love other than the unattainable *cosmic*, or Nature-type. At the time my father reached out to rescue me from la fortaleza, I wasn't capable of loving anything. No man, woman, child, country: no "thing." With his revelation, I began to feel freed from the prison of self-hatred, as well as the iron bars of that decrepit Dominican Republic jail cell he'd found me in. Gradually, trusting that love could heal me, revitalize me, I began learning to love my Self, and to trust humans again. Getting very quiet and spending time in Nature healed me, as She does to anyone who seeks Her solace.

The search for the ultimate in life suddenly shifted for me. No longer was I obsessed about discovering, then *having* the next thrill, conquest, or wild escapade. No longer was I driven to kill, maim or plunder to get a next fix of the lust-drug, that rush of orgiastic adrenalin, losing-control that lovemaking gives, or any other artificial high, for that matter.

Suddenly I suspected that real love—not the phony, superficial dime-a-dozen kind—had to be somewhere within myself. I was part of Nature, I figured. So therefore, I must be loveable. I'd heard enough about this from a host of enlightenment teachers to know that much.

Soon after the aircraft landed that brought us back to my family's hometown, I had a dream.

In which I found myself wandering an enormous, elegantly lavish mansion with shiny marble floors and walls, but with no windows at all. And no furniture either. I wandered the walled-in palace until I soon heard and came to find … a blue glowing figure who was melodically playing the flute. I floated toward the mysteriously beckoning creature, this long haired, luminous, darkly colored person, an androgynous looking, cerulean-browned being of some sort, who glowed charismatically.

"Who are you?" I whispered, standing before the tall, slim, umber-glowing, shimmering multi-hued person, who seemed at first completely ethereal, yet plainly as I came close, was as earthy as I was, as real to me as you or I. Scantily clad with only a loin cloth, I knew from the bare chest that this was a man. At least the top part of him was. He stopped playing his instrument, looked directly into my eyes, and spoke.

"You've been searching for me everywhere all your life, teZa."

"I have?"

"Now you know I'm right inside you. You and I, we're perfect lovers because we are One."

When I awoke, I happened to mention this dream to a friend, a fellow yogi who'd studied and practiced traditional Eastern meditation even before I began, years before this dream.

"Oh, that's that Blue Person," my friend knowledgeably proclaimed. "That's a textbook initiation dream; an awakening omen that happens to seekers on the path, the one you and I are on, and all of us who want to find the key so we can enter the not-so Secret Garden of Inner Peace. It's considered very auspicious to have a visitation from the Blue Person, who most definitely is your Higher Self. Only when a person is ready, it appears. Like an internal teacher, sort of. Only …" my girlfriend hesitated.

"Only what?" I asked, confusion mixing with gratitude upon hearing this; a mystical visit in a dream, considered a great boon to a seeker's journey—was that what my friend was saying?

"Only the Blue Person is supposed to appear to the seeker as the same sex they are. Yours is weird. You sure it was a man?"

From then on, I began to sense I *was* love. My Self. By doing the simplest of things, sitting on a sandy shore watching the waves roll in, one by one; smelling the fur of a floppy silly puppy; holding a newborn anything—I recognized pure Love in myself and in whatever I happened to be focusing on. Watching an inchworm hunch itself up a branch. Lying in bed listening to the awakening chirps of the many notes of different birds; noticing grunts and murmurs of creatures big and small as they nestled in for a good night's rest outside my open window.

Soon ... and with a purpose, because now I sought out the wisest teachers I could find ... I set out to heal the damaged places I had within. And shortly afterward—like magic it seemed—my true mate appeared.

After having nearly forgotten, I re-learned that Nature never gives up on us humans. Even though some of us appear lost and confused, some of us desperately look for answers to heal ourselves first, as each of us must do before we're any good for anyone else. If I could heal, or find better outlets than my negative compulsions—admittedly driven by wanting to dull the fear and emptiness that had been my sad companions, flinging myself on anything I mistook for love—if I could heal from this obsession of mine, anyone can heal from whatever is keeping them from experiencing wholeness.

I learned to substitute healthy habits for my unhealthy ones. Instead of having destructive tendencies, I now cultivated positive, healthy ones. Better diet, better friends, better subjects for the weird art I made. A dynamite man to love instead of just another loser or flake.

Anyone who wants to, can unlock their frozen, fear-stymied heart.

Listen to the wind. See the ice caps melting. Feel the cry of species disappearing, but remember, always remember with glad hearts, that new ones are being born at the same time. Yes, we grieve what is being lost, has already been lost, but we can also be assured that new species are always evolving, being discovered, replacing old ones that have not endured the challenges of changing times. Just as throughout all of history, change claims its victims as well as witnessing ever-adapting new creations. I had to accept that change is necessary, even if sometimes it might not appear as *good*.

Therefore, I had a choice: Instead of being locked in fear or sadness about the present, past or future, my heart could be filled with hopeful anticipation—if I but chose that.

Take this for-instance, to see what I mean. Just as how I was affected by my dad finally telling me about his tragic secret, when he revealed his boyhood's years-long abuse, so deeply shameful to him—it turned the tide for me in my own deeply troubled young life. We can all listen to our ancestors' woeful confessions, and understand that change is often accompanied by painful emotions. Change is inevitable, everyone must accept that. Listen to how our own Great Mother, the Earth is in pain. I shout Her message, the same one my father gave me about his own life:

"I've been hurt," I hear the Earth sing its mournful song. "And I've done some hurting of my own, children. But now it's time to change, so grieve no longer. Now's the time for both of us to focus on new ways. The time is here to let go of the old ways that brought only fear and suffering to so many of you."

Let's listen to our Great Mother, Gaia. Our world is crying as loudly, as clearly, as I'd heard my father relating his secret that day, when he confessed his hidden pain to me in the plane, returning home after rescuing me from my own private hell.

CHAPTER 3

pagan mama

F ar out to sea, the same pod of porpoises that once played with a tall, black-neoprene-clad human sister, are passing by the deeper waters off Sarasota. But they're not thinking of her, as she is of them. Unlike humanity, animals live in the present moment, each moment, every moment. Theirs is not a life of memories, intentions, or anticipations. Theirs is a life fully lived, even if it's just for this very second, this fleeting moment right here that we're in.

Each next moment too, is exactly right *Now*.

Even though the pod merrily plays and hunts, mates and interacts, each individual dolphin is only aware of that moment, right then.

This is why they appear to be such serene animals, and why so many of us are attracted to that stillness a playful dolphin emanates, from within.

In jagged sobbing heaves, five-year-old me awoke from a hellishly dank loneliness, sure that I was dead! What else could it have been?

Rushing into the kitchen where my folks sat talking late that night, I ran to them in my sweat-damp pajamas, screaming in holy terror.

"Mommy, mommy, I dreamt I'm dead! It was awful!" child-me wailed.

I'd gone to a painfully fearful place, just then. With only myself in the nightmare's macabre cast, I'd been taken to a very scary, dark region. Of course now, as an adult, I know that all places and characters in dreams actually are just our own self, costumed in many guises, reflecting our awareness of Being. This lightless place that scared me so, resembled nothing I'd seen before. Alone, feeling so small, so stifled, scared beyond anything I'd ever experienced, I was sure, absolutely sure, I bawled into Mama's ear, "I was dead! The dream killed me!" I wailed. "I feel I'm dead right now, this very minute!"

Perhaps that child I'd been had seen my first dead bird that day? Or a drowned worm left to dry in a leathery squiggle on a sunny pavement? Who can say? Because many memories of my early childhood are vague, fragmented: a common symptom of children who experience life-altering trauma, which wouldn't occur until years after the nightmare of this particular evening we're speaking of here.

"I'm going to die!" I shouted as I buried deeper into mother's ample arms, sure that the horror I'd dreamt was as real as the big comfort that embraced me now. Quieting somewhat, I sat on Mama's lap, heaving with fright, shivering in convulsions, surrounded by the strength and protective love of this woman named Eve.

"There there, little one," mother Eve cooed after hearing my disastrous dream explained. "Come back to bed with Mama and we'll fix everything."

She stood and carried me, her whimpering child, back to bed. Mother Eve had been born to Lithuanian immigrants and raised freely and wholesomely on that self-sufficient New Jersey hundred-acre farm I visited often. It had hardly a tie to outside influences other than the weekly bread truck delivery and the three kids, my mom and her siblings, who traipsed off to school when they were old enough, walking to the one-room brick building three miles away each morning, returning each afternoon, rain or shine, sleet or snow.

Lithuanians are a people that honor their pagan roots more than any other Roman Catholic culture does. The old-customs-honoring Lithuanian-Americans I know, more than any other Catholics, meet contemporary life's challenges with the additional aid of their Baltic myths that deal with human origins and destinies with intuitive, magical folktales, and other quaint customs. Christmas cookies shaped like mushrooms and ... *little ears?* Cookies or legends, all of them leftovers from their centuries-past original pagan roots, customs that eased modern living, making life a bit kinder for this last Eastern European country to embrace Christianity, by remaining faithful to both myths and tastes of earlier times.

As soon as an alternative concept enters the picture of the traditional heaven-hell-purgatory, reward-punishment, one-life-and-one-death orientation of mainstream Christianity—as in the Catholicism of my grandparents—things start getting interesting. When a Lithuanian like my mom, *Ave Maria*, the first born in her transported-to-America clan, lay close to dying, for instance, it would be proper and right for the soon-to-be-deceased to declare to their loved ones, what it was that they wanted their individual spirit to be reincarnated as, the ultimate wish list. Oak trees and bumblebees were popular choices in this category.

That night of my death-dream, when mama led me back to bed, my father, a large muscular man, whom Eve's peasant-style-farmer mother had dubbed, "Linwood, that Camden gangster," having suspected him of being a criminal merely because he was raised in a city and not on a farm, nodded to his more adept wife and stayed put at the linoleum-topped table where he was eating his nightly bowl of ice cream. Dad considered himself a Heinz 57 variety, as most Americans were at that time, the early fifties. His people had come from England on the second load of Pilgrims, in the seventeenth century. From Dad's side of the family I'm eligible to join the Daughters of the American Revolution, if I gave a hoot. From Mom's, I would learn the more enduring skills of coping with never-ending life challenges faced by first-generation immigrants, embracing America's uniquely collective modern soul. I learned the ways of Nature and grew close to animals through the benefit and advantage of my favorite person of all—my wise and peasant-minded, Lithuanian Grammmom, Antonina.

As Mama hoisted me up onto my rumpled bed, my older sister lay sleeping undisturbed in the twin bed next to mine. Still whimpering, though the gush of my tears had slowed, my head sunk into the softness of the damp pillow. Any word of comfort from a loving parent is a wave of soft healing to a child. I was blessed to have been born from two who adored their children as much as each other.

I lay in bed looking into those sea-green crystalline, compass-sionate eyes of my mother, so safe and assuring, and listened to her voice as my sniffles abated. Heaves of unknowns melted my stiff body into trusting this beautiful creature who was my protector, my nurturer, my private goddess: Mama.

"Close your eyes, Linduta," Eve said, using that endearing Lithuanian nickname she called her youngest. "Let's go to that horrible place you just were at and thought so scary."

"No Mama, no!" I cried, sitting fully up, tearing off the covers, renewing the flood of uncontrollable tears.

"Hush hush, little one. You have to trust me. Shush now, I'm going to show you there's absolutely nothing to fear."

Looking into mother's bright green eyes to make sure she wasn't playing a trick on me, I slowly laid back down, grabbing the soft blanket Eve put over me, clinging with my tight little fingers to the silky satin edge that I pulled up to my neck, afraid to let go.

"That's right, just close your eyes, Linduta. We're together. You're never alone. I'm here with you, always. Just close your eyes. Together let's go to that scary place you thought so terrible. Pretend you're back in that dream, right now, with me here with you. Don't worry. I won't go. Let's go to that same place that made you cry. Okay?"

I did my best to follow her instructions. I wanted to please her, yes, but I also somehow knew that *Mama knows what she's doing, because after all—she's Mama.*

"Are you back there now, Linduta?"

I nodded my head. I had slipped right back into that freshly felt, fear-filled place, that ugly dungeon of nothingness I had named death: Bad. Even though it had been terrifying, before—when my unconscious self brought that badness to the surface of my dream and mangled it into a nightmare—the child I was then, allowed herself to go back to that unsafe place—because Mama was instructing me to.

Here she is—I thought as I slipped between the worlds of wake and un-wake—*right beside me, protecting me.*

Fear of anything, in this moment mother and child shared so closely—was entirely forgotten.

I felt the warmth of mother's body come off her like a cookie-filled oven. The sweet spicy smell made me relax. I sank even deeper into the mattress. I felt the pressure of mama's gentle hand lightly patting the middle of my chest, as I lay deeply entranced by her whispered, soft entreaties. Listening to the musical lure of Mama leading me back to this unknowable, most fearsome state of all—the stillness of dark—it had to be death.

Eve sensed when her daughter drifted off asleep, noticing my body's limpness.

"Good," she said for only me and the Unseens to hear. "Now, Linduta, I want you to go even further back in your memories."

Sleeping now, I couldn't ask what Mama meant by that. Fast asleep, I heard, and followed Eve's guidance.

"Go further, follow your memories," she said. "Ease yourself back in time, little one. Allow yourself to be free to go wherever memories take you."

My sleeping child-self went. Deeply. Far away. My remembrances took me to a place that had neither colors or shapes, nor people or images, nor sounds or smells of any sort. It was a very light feeling, this place of unattached being-ness. I became aware of a swaying, swishing motion all around me, as if I were surrounded by a thick liquid.

"Are you there now, Linduta?"

I might have nodded my head, I didn't notice. My body was encased in a divinely sublime, watery trust. There was no effort, no muscular volition, no resistance from me whatsoever. My heart kept rhythmically beating. My tiny body-temple felt more alive, happier than I'd ever imagined possible in or out of dreams, knowing Mama was beside me like she was. I wouldn't recognize it until many years later, when I'd accrue enough vocabulary to match this inner experience with the outer world of acquired knowledge, but that state of watery-ness I was now experiencing was none other than ... remembering not-yet-born me floating inside my mother's womb! The evidence convinced me of this, in years to come.

"Good," Mama then said, blind to what her daughter was seeing or feeling, but sure of herself, her motives. "Now go back even further in your memories, Linduta."

Obediently, sleeping-me went. Deeper. Further into the strange byways of trust. Into a vastness that could only be described—again, by a word I would discover only years later—as bliss. Pure Joy.

In that state, I instantly sensed a feeling of utter completeness. A deliciously velvety peace. Time and space disappeared. I wasn't aware of being "me" or "I" or "separate from you." I felt only a totality, not being apart or separate from anything but ... *belonging* in a gigantic comforting way.

In that second-round, led-by-mom dream, there was no distinction from *me* and any other *It*—only a wholeness. In that dream place now, I was one with everything. Distinctly, I remember it like it was yesterday, I experienced the most tactile, definite sensation of being merged with All-ness, which was like nothing I'd ever experienced before, awake or asleep.

Was I asleep then? Maybe. Was this sensation a legerdemain of mother Eve's making? Done to replace her child's nightmare with a sweet dream? Who knows?

I vividly remember that event so long ago, even though so much else of my childhood is a big blank. In that wordless dream-place Mom led me to, I felt cared for, part of a complete whole. No different from my tender, safe surroundings.

No longer did I notice my mother's warm cookie smell, or hear the beating of her heart so close. She and I were no longer separate beings, as we had been when she brought me back to bed. Our hearts now beat in sync. And then—silence. Stillness. Nothing but safe secure Completeness. Absolute Peace.

A short while must have passed.

Then I dream-heard a distant voice. Mama was whispering to me, through the mist of my remembering.

"You see, my darling, that place you thought was being dead, was only you thinking death so scary, so foreign, so bad—but now you see, it's actually the place you came from before birth. Death, and before birth, they're one and the same thing, Linduta.

"There's never anything to fear. You *are* the energy of life repeating itself, little one. This is the sensation of pure Love, that you are."

you are the energy of life repeating itself, little one.

CHAPTER 4

the unlikely web of love you, hate you

In ancient legends surrounding the birth of the Buddha, sources claim all the animals made a pilgrimage to honor the Great Being. The Buddhist tale is similar to the biblical story of the Three Wise Men honoring Jesus' birth when they followed a star in the heavens, an omen everyone had been searching for. What they sought was the fulfillment of a prophecy, known for ages through legend, an event that would inevitably better all of humankind.

The animals en route to Buddha sensed a change was about to occur to the world, to humans and all that exists everywhere in the world. So they made their way, found a path to follow, and soon saw that all other animals from every corner of the world were converging, trudging their way as a group, toward the far off beacon of Light: the place of baby Buddha's birth.

As the crowd of animals approached the birthplace of this mythical baby Buddha (born already enlightened, in the legend), Mr. Rat joined the pack. "Oh Mr. Bull," Rat said to the giant bovine when he met him on the path, "I'm a small and tiny creature, can you please give me a ride upon your back?"

"Certainly," good-natured Bull said as Rat hopped onto the colossal being, joining the long line of other animals as they made their way to the Buddha's birthplace.

Finally, they saw the Light of Awareness guiding them to a

specific place. All the animals picked up the pace, including Mr. Bull with Mr. Rat upon his back. Amongst the animals—because these magical creatures chatted in one language, of course, as they made their pilgrimage—it was decided that whichever of them reached the newborn baby's side first would be crowned the smartest of them all. Every one of the creatures, big or small, picked up the pace, wanting that noble distinction.

Just as the giant Mr. Bull rushed past all the others, gaining on even the cheetah (who had a sore paw and was limping badly) and the horse (who stopped to eat some tasty grass along the roadside) … Mr. Rat could see from the Light that shone above that they were almost at their final destination,

Suddenly, within eyesight of accomplishing the feat of being first at Buddha's side, Rat rushed down the lowered neck of Bull, who had stooped from fatigue to rest for just a moment. Rat hopped onto the ground and ran with all his might straight to the baby's side.

"I'm first, I'm best! I'm the smartest!" Mr. Rat yelled, arriving at the infant's side giddy with himself instead of humbly bowing to the mythical newborn.

And this is why the wily rat, reviled by some, is considered to be the smartest in the Animal Kingdom to this very day.

Love and hate come in all ways, shapes, and forms.

Native Americans say, "What we do to One, we do to All. We exist in the *Web of Life.*"

My longtime pal Mike and I used to delight in belting out "Love you, hate you!"—the silliest line in an otherwise heart-wrenching Shirley Basset torch song. Mike and I had been sailing buddies, our end-of-day beer-swilling chorus a hilarious and fun sort of ritual that we enjoyed while chugalugging Greenies (Heineken beer), sitting in either of our two boat's cockpits that were anchored nearby one another in the lagoon of St. Thomas. Those lyrics "Love you! Hate you!" didn't make *any* sense to us. We just loved the ridiculous sound of them, as ludicrous as "Kill me! Kiss me!" Back then, both Mike and I were at the height of our wild-child adventuring. Separately cruising the latitudes of various Caribbean islands on sailboats or cargo vessels, enjoying our unattached lusts, our freedom to roam, including the unlimited easy-Customs entry to the laid-back ports that were the norm in those less dangerous, way more accessible times, before September 11, 2001 put an end to free and easy border crossing.

Mike and I were close friends of the same tribe, lovers of ocean wind and comfortable self-reliance. Each of us was a gypsy traveler on the high seas, searching for the next adventure, unafraid to follow steady trade winds as much as our strong gut instincts.

Then, years flashed by. No longer did I drink beer, or sail the seas, but was raising a blended family, a whole gang of lovers surrounding me in place of another loner like myself.

The years of concentrated kid-raising finally came to a completion when our kids graduated from college, and I had time to reflect on things other than preparing the next meal, attending the next soccer match, sacrificing the next, the next, whatever kid-or-husband-or-career demand came next.

The mantra of a family person.

The Age of Reason that we all must reach, more like Mr. Bull, not as much in a rush as his companion who was determined to be best, the first, the *most*, like Mr. Rat did, rushing ahead, had finally come to me.

What I was finally ready to *see*, was how I now understood that our entire species of humankind is a blended family, like my own is. And right now we humans, in our worldwide dysfunctional family scenario, are at the adolescent stage, the most awkward crossroad of our evolutionary journey thus far. Much like Mr. Bull and Mr. Rat on the journey to the Light of Awareness.

Love you, hate you. Love me or hate me, believe me or laugh at my foolishness … none of it matters.

You, me, all of us human beings, combined—we are barely out of our species' sprout-stage, our collective infancy. On the slow-mo timeline of past/present/future, the immediate right here and *Now*, is the summation of all previous possibilities all rolled into this *one instant*, right here. Every "right here" is the magic moment of *the Now*. And then there's a next one, a completely new Now. Just as every one of us is part of our combined blended human family, each of our individual experiences is as meaningful, as necessary an element in the continuity of our entire civilization. Each of our lives represents a whole-ness, yet each of our individual lives is essential, meaningful—and necessary to the overall story of humankind's evolution. Yet we're also as ridiculously insignificant as that facetious old drinking song of Mike's and mine: just as nonsensical to think about as singing "Love you, hate you!" in the same beery, illogical phrase. Yet each of us enjoys wasting our time and energy bickering over such inane trivialities as we do, every day, on the internet, in the political arena, surrounding our sound-and-screen circus with such nonsense as we do.

We must all remember *to not* be like Mr. Rat and rush rush—to where? To an empty, bewildering legend that may or may not even exist. Instead, let's refocus that leap of Rat-like impulsive action— to a place deep within ourselves. At the end of the day, Mr. Bull, tired but truly sturdy on his feet, is making his way to the same beacon of light as Mr. Rush Rush Rat did. Who cares who comes first? No one cares!

At this most awkward stage of our species' evolutionary development, which we've arrived at after hurdling over the agricultural and industrial revolutions, we are now in an intellectually superior era in which we're poised to create AI, robots and bio-engineered entities of all sorts to take over our day-to-day menial tasks.

We must not be over-reacting, evolutionary teenyboppers, like Mr. Rat was.

Let's savor this in-between stage, and try to accept others, instead of judging people as being right or wrong, bad or good, hatefully self-centered or lovingly compassionate. Let's strive to be more like the Buddha than either Bull or Rat.

The overall balance of people who hate, compared to already awakened hearts (whom I call hybrid vigors), people who love unconditionally, points to the truth that Love champions over senseless Hatred; or, as I prefer to call hate by its *real* name: Fear.

History has proven, over and over, that acceptance of *the new* is intrinsic to change, and when the opening of the human heart happens to one person at a time, the natural consequence is the inevitable expansion of the entire human species' collective perceptions, or consciousness. Over time, tolerance of the New gets accepted by every generation. Humanity learns from repetition, how to combat evil. Each reign of terror, each "Bad" event transforms us, in time, always, into something greater, something more highly evolved: something "Good."

Before, when I used to mindlessly sing, "Love you, hate you!" with Mike, I never bothered to think about such things. I wasn't concerned about loving or hating. I was just living. I was experimenting. I was gathering experiences.

And then, I changed. I put down my wild self-destructive ways. I chose to marry and take on responsibilities of raising two young children with my soul match, once I found him. Everything changed when I experienced that alteration of my perceptions: when I had to become responsible.

Patience, Understanding, and Acceptance are the old aunties of everyone's family, reminding us that, in time, Love wins over hate.

After leaving my birth family, I never thought I'd *ever* be interested in embracing another family. There'd been too many frustrations, too much work to rise up from the ashes of my bruising childhood What I didn't realize until ready to have a family of my own, is that every family—whether a group of humans or a family-unit comprised of one person alone, or with a pet, say, or only with a comforting TV or screen as companion—provides exactly what each soul needs to achieve their particular variety of experiences. For what? To feel completely in Love, with Love.

Love is what's needed for soul growth.

It took healing myself, first, from the senseless, illogical disease of self-destructive addiction before I would ever be able to recognize unconditional love when it came knocking at my door. I had to almost die several times, before stubborn-me could accept the need to nurture my shattered Self.

Now I can sense how Earth's global challenges are evolving in a similar, parallel manner as all fractured lives do, that are becoming whole again. We are microcosms of the macrocosm. Now I am part of the helping-others-to-heal tribe, we survivors who have found a way to become whole, after our inner Selves became diminished, through one means or another.

I began my journey of acceptance by choosing to stop self-destructing. I had to get sober to do this, and afterwards, I got to help others. I assisted both my parents' spirits, sat at their side as each left behind their body, thirty years apart. I had the privilege of walking my immediate forebears to the gate that separates both worlds, the Seen and the Unseen, and say, "Good bye, fare thee well" to their individual lights, as each of my biological parents joined the realm of the Unseens.

Tolerance and compassion are the teachers that showed me how to accept my ancestral roots. Now I can clearly see my role. I am a bridge to the unseen realm, a role I earned from having helped my stranded, bewildered-at-the-end parents.

What I'm saying is no more far-fetched than the crazy reality that surrounds all of humankind today: extreme entertainment and sports, massacres done to innocents in schools, not just in wartime or zones; people numbing themselves with legal and illegal drugs. Nature offers the most conspicuous ways of announcing the urgency for people to quickly change: natural extremes such as global weather changes; folks claiming mixed or fluid gender identities in head-turning numbers, some of them switching back and forth with ease and satisfaction. Every soul's personal identity is now only restricted by one's imagination, or one's ability to speak honestly from their heart.

When Nature is thrown off balance, She compensates. Overpopulation has resulted in a natural shift in humanity's identifying with our being more than mere physical entities. Our identity is shifting from material to spiritual, as naturally as a snake sheds its skin. For some people, a shift in their personal sexual identification can occur—just as it commonly does among too tightly growing crops of plants and overpopulated herds or flocks of animals— because Nature always compensates for overgrowth. We switch gears, allegiances of affection just as other biological and botanical species have always done. Nature always acts in accordance with seeking to maintain equilibrium, the give and take of creation.

Humans, naturally, follow the lead of Nature's tendencies.

Nature's true name is Love. Humans who suffer from overdoses of fear and suffer from imbalances have forgotten this.

Today I awoke from a dream I've never dreamt before. In it, a group of people and I were hiding, fearing for our lives. We were under attack by a lone angry madman with a gun, an all too common scenario in our imbalanced, nonsensical world of today.

I awoke asking myself: What am I, personally, doing about the widespread fear so many suffer from in today's crazy world? What must I do to remember that breath itself is my life's anchor, and all I have—is right Now?

I asked my Self these things and this is the reply I got:

When fears are brought out into the open, they die. Things of darkness shrivel and fade away from the Light of Love. Love is being conscious. Love is awareness. Love is the cure of all dis-ease.

That's what these different facets of Love I'm honored to be sharing with you are about. Various aspects of elevated Love. Sharing such things with you is needed because I'm now dedicated to being a more whole, more balanced version of the lesser person I used to be.

The better version of a person is called by many names, some majestic or sacred, still others, clinically complex. Hybrid vigors call the better, higher consciousness known as the Divine, simply Love.

Back when I did scientific illustrations of plants, it was a botanist who taught me what a hybrid vigor is.

"If you take two plants of the same species," Tim explained to me early in our collaboration, "both of which prominently exhibit far superior, desirable qualities more pronounced than any others in that species—hardiness after a fruit's maturity, for example, or ease of germination when seedlings are transported to various climes— and we cross pollinate these two hardy specimens, their offspring, their seeds will produce a new and better, vastly improved version of the same species, with those superior qualities the parent-plants manifested. This new plant and its fertile seed is the hybrid vigor, a completely *new subspecies* of the parent stock."

CHAPTER 5

we are one

A snake has much to offer. We know how one such no-legged creature wreaked havoc on the world of humanity, according to a garden story described in Genesis. But there is another significant way how Snake has influenced our human brothers and sisters. Its very shape presents, to many who choose to dwell on such things, a deepened understanding of what existence itself is all about.

The ancient symbol of a snake with its tail in its mouth, called *ouroboros* by the Greeks, the continuously infinite interior-space created within the tail-eating snake itself, referred to by the ancients as "the golden egg" or "the golden womb" (the *hiranyagarbha* written about in the sacred Vedas of Hinduism) signifies the never-endingness of consciousness, of Life itself, before, during and beyond the earthly, physical realm. A snake sheds its skin. Continuously giving re-birth to itself, anew, reinventing itself into something much better.

Snake has much to show us. And please, do remember to put a big distance between yourself and any poisonous or large constricting serpent.

Snake in the grass is sometimes mistaken for a slippery omen, a sign of danger.

As a common folktale so aptly puts it, a person walking down the road at night who's not awake yet (not yet tapping the unlimited capabilities of human potential), could jump back terribly frightened at seeing a snake in the middle of a dark path. Yet upon closer inspection … it turns out to be merely a piece of rope.

We along the road to discovering a better, more sustaining manner of living in union with others, all critters, as well as our physical surroundings, know this much: Things are not what they appear to be.

A coiled snake with its tail in its mouth is something you'll rarely see in Nature but frequently in artistic renderings (ancient, classical, modern artworks, books on symbols, as well as ink on bodies these days). The ouroboros is a sign of … eternality ….

Throughout my life I've experienced a mysterious mirror-like connection between myself and all others, between all beings—all things, in fact. Trees and bees and my indigenous blood-sister, our pact made with swapped blood drawn by a safety pin when both us girls were nine years old. She was the daughter of my mother's housecleaner, as much my pal as the creatures all around her. Bernice and I recognized our sameness instantly.

Imagine my surprise and confusion then, when I reached adolescence and discovered something experienced by others, but had remained unknown to me up till then. I didn't know what to call this harsh feeling, this kick in my gut. In time, I heard it called xenophobia, and discovered it was rampant in my small Midwestern town, as it was throughout most of America at that time. People were suspicious after having lost so many dear ones during the Second World War.

Being separate from "others" was real to some even in my own family. This was the exact opposite from feeling One-with-everything I experienced in my younger years. Later, when I discovered that some people combined prejudice and exclusion with how they chose to worship at churches, synagogues, temples, or social clubs—I was so disappointed, shocked, and incredulous. How could everything *not* be God, I wondered, even when someone like a so-called *bad person*—a drunk, a prostitute, a homosexual, they said—all be equivalent to paid assassins and cutthroat pirates? Judgment of others confused me.

I became confused when others told me I had to exclude and separate things into categories outside of "all things are created by God." So, I rebelled. The underlying thread of my young existence—of sensing the obvious unity among all things—could not be dispelled by rules, scoldings, or threats of damnation issued by the laws of my family's religion, for things as nonsensically disparate as French-kissing a boy or committing murder. I decided to seek out answers for myself. I'd go beyond the scope of my family, its designated religion, my own American culture if I had to, to get some answers.

Only after I'd exhausted a true devotion to the religion of my upbringing—in which I found, besides the more attractive mysteries and rituals, many obstacles, annoying paradoxes and confounding hypocrisies at every bend along the bumpy road of searching for my own beliefs—did I seek out what was then, in the sixties, called nontraditional paths, or Eastern mysticism.

My personal search took me to many teachers, some not alive, some not from Western culture. Some not even human.

Thus began my deep discipleship with Nature.

The sea taught me perhaps more (in a non-verbal manner of course) than any other guide I ran across as I set out on the road to find my own Truth. Not *other people's truth.* In every clime and continent, natural settings of the world reached out to me to reinforce my suspicions that there is an invisible union between All in existence. All one has to do to prove this is observe how Nature is: day in, day out, weekly, monthly, yearly, in and through natural cycles, both short and widespread.

Everywhere I looked, mountaintops, deserts, or oceans, weather events united with earth-water-sky like wild herds of rampaging cosmic beasts, trumpeting and stampeding when aroused; becoming gentle playful kittens when disruptive systems fizzled out, coming to peaceful rest once again.

Everywhere I looked, I saw that Nature spoke Truth, at least the kind I could understand, much more sensibly demonstrated than by my school's, church's, government's, or parents' rules ever did.

All children sense the wondrous union of Nature, even if their parents have forgotten, or hampered themselves from knowing. Kids experience and remember, but only a rare adult can recall how they sensed Oneness when they were children, when Carefree was their religion. Before clamps got a chance to be placed over perceptions, over wide-open, feeling hearts. Children sense the joy of first raindrops on their upturned faces, the magic of watching a bee flitting among blossoms, the up-close majesty of a small blade of grass, the kinship one feels with a far-off star—just as I did and you probably felt, as every youthful heart experiences. Young kids are ever mindful of Nature as the greatest Teacher of All, the Source of strength, the Font of fascination. In adolescence, I let Nature direct me from inside my heart to focus on this sensation of unity—and never listened to the adults claiming separation and judgment of others that I found so suspicious and—well, downright sacrilegious.

I decided to listen to Nature, not the other, dissonant sources all around me.

In time, I came to fully accept, intuitively first, then eventually, intellectually, but only after feeling in a visceral, unspeakable fashion, this universal Truth—the feeling of all-as-One. I subjected this *all-is-One,* or unity, or as I simply say—*It*—to many tests. Today, having tested *It* ad infinitum (and heard some of the other thousands of *Its* names), I choose to nurture and share in whatever way I can, this comforting worldview: that we, you and me, and all in existence are united, like individual cells, within the wholeness of *It.*

Many others feel this same Truth as I do, and live according to *It.* Unity consciousness has become one of humankind's most cherished, energetically peace-bestowing attributes of our species. I myself work as hard to focus on the Joy of *It* as some work on their six-pack abs at the gym, or their professional studies, their social media posts, sports moves, or culinary skills. Naturally, as an artist I began writing and arting about this subject so close to my heart, the unity-of-all, ages before meeting my art mentor, H. As soon as I'd developed the required acumen by which I could express the meaning of my existence, I began to envision how to express *It*.

And then—just as I was beginning to explore depicting *It* in my art work—the most amazing thing happened!

Instead of operating on blind faith, concerning *It,* I was given the most startling and tangible proof about the unity of *All* in existence, when the most phenomenal thing occurred. A precious gift was handed to me by my own similarly lifelong-questioning father, Linwood. He was a man who'd always wanted to believe in some higher purpose of being alive … but he too, had needed proof before he could honestly say he *believed* in *It*.

My own beloved father got to experience *It* for himself, and I was there as his witness.

Dear ol' Dad was approaching the portal that separates this world from what lies beyond, but … he wasn't ready to go quite yet. He looked away from me—who sat at his bedside, waiting, watching, listening—toward where he saw the Truth. Eventually, he came back to tell me himself, what he'd experienced. Time stood still, as he quietly struggled to get each word out, but finally, he managed to distinctly say to me, looking deeply into my eyes with every bit of assurance a daughter ever can get from her father when she's in need—to me alone he plainly spoke, amazed and aloud:

"It really is true: We are all One," he said, as factually as if stating, *It's true, humans are all bones, flesh and blood.* "What a shame," he continued, "some people don't get to know it until too late."

... never-endingness of consciousness, of Life It-self ...

A little while later, a look of wondrous peace washed over my father's face. I was repeating to him the words he'd spoken to me just a short while before. Somehow, he'd forgotten saying them, because, you see, he hadn't been in his "right mind" when he saw, and became enraptured visiting the invisible realm to which he was himself then headed.

The same realm where all the Unseens reside, they tell me. Where some of us, who want to, can go back and forth, using the bridge from one realm to the other that each of us erects when we attune our consciousness to our peaceful breathing.

"Dad," I quietly said, "you just told me, 'We are all One' like you were seeing it for yourself—without a doubt. I was watching you, and it was as if you were experiencing something extraordinary that very moment," I now reported back to him, "when you said, 'We are all One.'"

At first Linwood looked completely bewildered by my words. Then—astounded! He blinked and mumbled, "Really, I said that?"

I said, "Yes, Dad, I think you were just visiting wherever it is that your spirit is soon heading for."

Dad looked like he understood what I was saying. That pleased me no end, to repeat his own words for my ever-skeptical, agnostic dad. His face, pale against the white pillow he laid upon, registered understanding. His body seemed to suddenly relax, to surrender to gravity, after hearing my bedside report eagerly given back to him, of the extraordinary experience he'd just told me that he had had. I could see he trusted my words, my reporting back to him what he'd reported to me. I repeated for his edification (knowing what a spiritual wonderer he'd always been) his own testimony of Oneness.

"It's really true, you'd said, Dad." Figuring it would comfort him, knowing this Oneness he'd spoken of is where he was about to merge back into, as an Unseen, back to the shared dimension of reality we Seens all originate from, only many of us too often forget.

As Dad fell into a peaceful slumber, his words, "… some people don't get to know it until too late," kept ringing in my ears. *It isn't*

45

too late for Dad, now. I smiled to myself, happy for my father that he got to experience, while still in his human form, what he actually is—pure Spirit—but had only forgotten, like so many of us do.

I silently kept repeating, absolutely wonder-struck: *Thank you Dad, for this gift. This gift of insight you've given me. It's proof positive of what I've suspected my entire life. That everything—is connected, somehow, as Oneness.*

I sat beside my father, feeling elated, glowing with this final gift of his. Finally, I'd been handed proof of what everyone always thinks so esoteric, ineffable, improbable—the eternalness, the interconnectedness of all in existence. Always before, I had found answers to my cosmic questioning from mystic artist-writers, such as Kahlil Gibran, William Blake, or from reading early scriptural texts of yoga, Taoism, and Buddhism. As I sought spiritual teachers, all the good ones always confirmed Jesus the Christ's message: *The kingdom of God is within you.* Yet so few of my peers had I ever been able to talk to about this subject, my longing to know true Love, the Divine within all. I'm sure many, especially from the art world, regarded my work as non-mainstream, non-commercial, and obsessed about unseen energies, my favorite subject. I tried to visualize or conceptualize the interconnectedness of all beings, considered out-there stuff at every gallery or art dealer I ever approached, but the only concept I considered worthy of focusing on in my studio work.

I sat beside him, my hard-working, now decade-long sober father, dying from cancer. Now, at the very end of his life, he was handing me the missing link that would direct and fuel my life's path, and my work, from then on. Linwood's never-to-be-denied words of the Truth about Oneness would assure me for the rest of my days that I wasn't crazy.

I could trust this personal belief I had, how connected we all are, from that moment on.

When my father slipped into, for real, that same flight pattern he'd already checked out—and had relayed to me in his awed state of witnessing Oneness, reporting as he had to me what he'd seen and felt—in just a few hours more he would cross the barrier between this world, what came before it, what comes after it, to wherever he was headed, where we're all headed: where the Unseens reside. Linwood went peacefully. His comfort had been handed to him by me, his grown, sober-now daughter. With a serene smile on his translucent face, alit with wonder and anticipation, Linwood left his worn out, diseased body with no regrets. He was euphoric to join the Oneness. He was ready.

The last thing he said to me, was whispered before he slipped past the veil that separates the Seen from the Unseen:

"Even though I'll be changed, I'll always be with you. I'll be here to help you whenever you need me."

He took a deep, long breath, mustering the energy to say his last words on Earth.

"I promise you, sweetheart, it's true: Love is what we are. Love is pure energy."

CHAPTER 6

we are but guests of nature

A bee hovers near its target. Gathering nourishment for its tribe back at the hive. Its wings furiously beat the air as it suspends, looking for the plumpest, most fragrant, juiciest feast of pollen-laden nectar in its sight. Its thousand-lens eyes seeing front, behind, all sides, up, down, and yet it only takes a split second for the bumbling creature to make the perfect choice. It comes closer to the sweet-smelling blossom, one of millions, yet the most perfect for that moment. The bee rests, nestling, sucking, bouncing on the blossom's cheeks, its protruding straw-like proboscis gathering nectar, drop by drop, until the next fully laden treasure beckons. The bee takes off, delighted to have such a role in the fabric of this world, feeding the whole of Bee Nation with each of its tiny sucks.

A collective effort, one this bee was born to participate in as a gatherer, nothing more, nothing less. Its ancestors refined these abilities to such perfection it now is … performing its role, doing its drone job honorably. Living its dharma, this bee: providing nourishment and survival for the collective colony. When I held the bee, so much smaller than me, in my trusting, childhood hands, I never thought of being harmed. And never got harmed, in turn. I, a child doing her experimenting-dharma as much as the bee gathering nectar was, held it gently in my cupped, trusting palms.

A phone call rang in my East Hampton cottage. From New Zealand, from Hundertwasser, my longtime mentor, H.

"Come to Opua, won't you, teZa. Just you and me. No promises, no strings. Just making art like we do so well. We can work side-by-side, you and I. Protect our creative gifts from the harsh, cruel world outside. We'll sail *Regentag* around the Bay of Islands, and when we're here in my jungle, we'll live in *Ao Tea Roa*, eat fiddleheads and wild mushrooms we pick ourselves when we're not working on our art, side by side."

It took only a few loud heartbeats of silence upon hearing H's unexpected proposal to know my answer. "Thanks, Friedrich, but I'm going to have to pass on that very tempting, very gracious offer."

My buzzing heart had been speaking of other things, other needs, other callings than isolating from the things I loved about the world, things I knew Friedrich cared not a bean for. Friedrich (the name he asked me to call him, but to others I call him *H* for Hundertwasser) intensely disliked noisy children, dancing, jokes, and music of any sort. His world was a bubble of his own aesthete-making. If people or events weren't absolutely attuned to the peacefulness, the grandeur of aesthetics, the unparalleled beauty of unadorned Nature—Friedrich simply wasn't interested. He demanded as much from those around him as he himself strove for: perfection, he'd softly admonish me in years past whenever we visited, whether in the Caribbean, Vienna, or that one time in New York City. How else, he'd say, could he make his caliber of *High Art*?

The biggest test of my life, up to that date, on the day when H called from halfway around the globe, from his home in Opua, was for me to say "No" to something I'd always thought was my destiny. H was supposed to be perfect for me, didn't I remember? To stand there with the phone in my hand and, without any hesitation, say "No" to H inviting me to New Zealand, would have been un-thinkable not so very long before. Before I'd taken that awful old work of mine to the dump. Before I'd put down the drinking and drugging. Before—I met Will. Everything was different, now that I was awakening to what Love really was, who I really was.

"I simply can't, Friedrich," I explained in response to his asking why not. "When I last saw you, I certainly would have jumped at this chance. Time has changed me; my priorities are different now. Truthfully, I think I'm in love with a man who's an artist like us, but he can live in the real world, too. I know how much you hate the real world. Will has children, so I'm not rushing into anything yet. I'm not even sure he's good for me. But I'm thinking about it. He has an extended, wonderfully complex, smart and sophisticated family scene. Everything about him is attractive to me, except of course, the step-mothering business. He's a single-parent. With full custody. Talk about *work,* kid-style. Thank you so much for the invitation, Friedrich. Will and I haven't even talked about being together, not yet. Still, after meeting him a couple months ago, I can't just run away from these strong feelings. I have to check them out. I have to pay attention to my heart."

"As you wish, my dear," H said in his nonchalant, Viennese monotone.

It was the same tone he always used to address collectors, dignitaries, fishermen, or farmers. The same droning, non-committal voice he also used to read his proclamation about human rights when he was honored at the United Nations that time I joined him, when he was celebrated for designing those commemorative stamps.

In his speech that year, at the U.N. headquarters, I proudly listened as H softly proclaimed:

"Postage stamps are the measure of the cultural standing of a country. The tiny square connects the hearts of the sender and the receiver, reducing the distance. They represent a bridge between people and countries. The postage stamp passes all frontiers ...."

He paused briefly. No sound came from the packed audience. He looked directly at me as I stood facing him, among hundreds of others, and nodded, a private sign between us in the array of distinguished notorieties. He continued.

"That is why I salute this noble endeavor of the United Nations to present stamps of such unique meaning, because who else should, and must, give a shining example to the world for a better life on Earth in beautifulness, in harmony with the creativity of Nature and man, if not the United Nations ... where the longings of all people meet."

That day H presented his stamps commemorating six Freedoms of Human Rights that he had chosen himself, to honor with his recognizable naturalistic, brightly colored designs. Slowly and clearly enunciating in strongly accented English, he read from his prepared papers.

"*The Right* of a Peace Treaty with Nature ... We are but guests of Nature," H read his own words, "and we must behave. Humans must admit that they, each one, is the most dangerous pest that ever devastated the Earth." He hesitated a moment before introducing his next Freedom.

"*The Right* to Dream ... Dreams are the last kingdom where humankind can take refuge and recover. Taking dreams away from each individual in a rationalistic society is a crime because dreams are the precondition of creation." Again, he paused, and then read on.

"*The Right* of The Second Skin ... If the second skin of a person, their clothes, is uniform, made by soulless machines or dictated by fashion, it will be like a false skin, like a foreign body." H allowed a moment of silence before proceeding.

"The Window *Right* ... Every person must have the right to lean out of their own window as far as their arms can reach so that that person distinguishes themselves from their imprisoned neighbors, so that from far away everybody can see: there lives a free person." Again, a moment of silence.

"*The Right* to Create ...," H began to read tenderly. "Creation is the foremost human condition. Our real illiteracy is not the incapability to read and write, but the incapability to create. The children and the so-called primitive and the so-called fool have bigger knowledge to create, until they lose their soul by uniform-ation and convention." He ended in a stronger voice, and looked around the entire audience before reading the last of his six Free-doms.

"*The Right of* ... Homo Humus Humanitas ... The right and duty of humankind to be reborn and to perpetuate on this earth by means of ... recycling their own waste. By means of humus toilets producing humus." H stopped, looked up for a brief moment, and made a sweeping glance of the commotion arousing all around him, and then continued. "With burial proceedings in harmony with the laws of Nature, where our dead are transformed into trees planted on the graves. And a recovery of agriculture and human activities at all levels away from poison, destruction and monoculture."

H took off his reading glasses, and quickly left the podium.

Pandemonium erupted! The room broke into a quivering rumble, drowning out H's final vowels and consonants. Everyone gasped at this last Freedom of his that H had intentionally chosen to present last for the revered, notoriously conservative institution. All around me, upset people were whispering, shaking their heads in horrified disbelief.

In his unassuming manner, H had just announced what to most people's senses, was strictly off-limits, a taboo subject. The last stamp commemorating a Freedom of his choice that H introduced, depicted by his whimsical, signature motifs of spirals and shiny metallics, honored bodily functions no polite company was prepared to hear mentioned, leastwise honored. My eccentric, eco-warrior mentor had announced his personal choices of essential Freedoms; the personal creed by which he lived, his friends knew all too well. The last one he mentioned, it turned out, was nothing short of abhorrent to the overdressed group of international representatives.

I heard someone close to me in the disrupted audience loudly say, "He can't be a *successful* artist. Look at those clothes! Disgraceful!"

Exactly. That's why I knew H included *dressing as one pleases* for one of his Rights, because of how people judge one another from outer appearances instead of seeing each other's Light within.

After H's speech, instead of thunderously approving applause, I heard nothing but shocked commotion and confusion in the standing-room-only reception area. I looked around and saw grimacing, alarmed people rushing to leave, turning to each other mumbling, "He must be crazy!" "Did he just say what I think he said?" "Is he talking about—it can't be!—recycling human feces and—good God!—dead human bodies buried to feed tree roots?!"

I stood silent and alone. From across the great hall's bouncing sea of bobbing heads, H looked right into my eyes, nodding agreement to what we both knew was the good shock everybody there needed, but hadn't planned on receiving. Surprises are uncomfortable for dignitaries of all nations. Both of us couldn't help chuckling as we made our way to each other's side, hearing the outrage, seeing the waters of humanity part wide, as H walked toward me.

H upsetting the status quo, again, I thought. H's official trick on this crowd of stuff-shirts was no surprise to me. I knew his history, how he'd been one of the earliest demonstrators to bring people's awareness to the environmental crisis, back in the late fifties and early sixties. I knew how much he loved pulling the rug from under the establishment's feet. And yes, next to Great Art, I knew recycling human shit was H's most favorite subject of all.

Everywhere H lived, certainly all the places I'd visited him— his fancy rooftop studio in Vienna, his deep-water sailing vessel when we first met in the West Indies—he'd installed a humus toilet, insisting visitors bend to using his preference of no-water, organic recycling of their own waste. Whenever he designed a structure (he was equally famed for his large-scale architecture as he was for his readily available fine art prints) whether a multiple residential apartment or industrial building, he introduced the necessity of recycling and the ultimate of that—using humus toilets. Whether a client chose water plumbing or a self-contained, human waste-recycler installed upon request, that decision was left to each of his many buildings' occupants.

Yes, H was obsessed with recycling shit, just as I'd been with discovering Love. His studied, ardent interests demonstrated the extent of his commitment to environmentalism, just as my own efforts, including a lifelong duty of recycling and composting that helped me to become a better person, a more caring world citizen. As everyone knows, recycling is at the top of the list of how best to conserve the Earth's resources. At the top of H's recycling list was compost toilets.

Years before the U.N. event, H had published manifestos about his passions, publicly declaring his conservation activism in Europe, since the Second World War ended. As sought after as his Nature-honoring artistic creations, H's environmentalism was widespread and controversial. H made fine art history in the field of reproductions by printing the unheard-of amount, of up to five thousand, of his silkscreen works at a time when editions of more than a few hundred were considered gauche and low-brow.

A Jewish child of Nazi oppression, whose clever mother hid him from the Nazis in Vienna, in full view, by forcing him to pose as one of Hitler's youth corps, H became a man sworn to midwife a new era of unity consciousness and worldwide conservation. He made a peace-heralding modern version of a united Semitic flag, featuring both the Arab crescent and Jewish star, seen wherever he could convince people to fly it, and meant to inspire the two camps to end their age-old conflict.

It's a toss-up, about which is the most shocking of his non-art, written offerings: his treatises on "Humus Toilet," or "Free Nature is our Freedom," or, my personal favorite, H's published manifesto on recycling: "Shit Culture—Holy Shit."

The influence of his posters—*Save the Seas* and *Save the Whales*—seen all over Europe, the profits of which H donated to the radical efforts initiated by Greenpeace, caused the world to take note of the mid-twentieth-century revolutionary Green Movement. H's popularizing the nascent grassroots politicos with his usual combo of bold art mixed with a healthy dose of his favored, bare-naked-shock factor, is thought to have been largely attributable to Greenpeace's worldwide fame.

Ten years previous to his inviting me to join him in New Zealand, I had received a telegram from H. My longtime friend had wired me to request I accompany him to the annual U.N. commemorative event in New York City.

I sipped only water from the tall thin-stemmed glass I was offered, having newly sworn off booze. I hoped my excitement didn't look too preposterous on me. My height allowed me to hover over the distinguished crowd, proud to be the companion of the most environmentally active artist of the day. In my downtown Manhattan artist duds, black boots and tights and slinky black velvet sheath I'd made practically overnight for the occasion, I knew H preferred a statuesque woman standing by his side, mimicking how his adored mother, Elsa had been. This wouldn't be the most outlandish event I'd ever attend with H, just the most public.

Still, that springtime phone call, ten years later, inviting me to New Zealand became a notable cairn on my journey to self-awakening, as significant as when H telegrammed me requesting me to join him at the U.N. on such short notice. From clinging to his every word, to hearing myself say "No" to his invitation to join him, artist-to-artist, I had to ask myself, *What has changed so much about me?* Before, I'd have jumped at any chance to be with my dear H. Saying *No* to H's offer, of his unexpectedly inviting me to join him *to live and work* with him at his isolated, semi-tropical jungle home, was me truly claiming: "I've reset my life's goals."

Declining his offer, in itself, isn't so very interesting. But the fact that long before that phone call arrived, I'd decided my true destiny was to be none other than as *Mrs. H ...* that *No* of mine became the most pronounced cairn along my journey of discovering Self Love.

Ten years before that *No*, enticing mail and teasing, half-honest invitations had come from him regularly, ever since the perfect sunshiny day H maneuvered his astonishing red-sailed Regentag into the harbor of Grenada's St. George's. He was on his way to New Zealand for the first time. He'd sailed from Europe some weeks before, joining his boat's captain and crew for the transatlantic crossing. We met on his first day in Grenada, where I was working on an early Arawak and Carib Indian display for the island's national museum. After meeting on a dock, as sailors tend to do, we became inseparable during the entire time H was in Grenada. Afterwards, whenever he wrote cryptic, caring notes to me as he traveled around the world, painting wherever he stayed, exhibiting his psychedelic-like work (oxymoronic for one who never imbibed *anything*) in major art centers everywhere, he always ended his far-flung missives, scratched on postcards, sealed with exotic postal stamps, ending with the same weirdly noncommittal tease: "One day we'll be together."

Over the ensuing years before his for-real invitation to join him arrived, no matter where he or I travelled, H's affectionately scribbled notes and occasional multi-paged letters, had weaned down to every once in a long while. Yet, like a parrot repeating its scant repertoire of well-programed, choice words, H tormented me with those pat, emotionless catch-phrases of his that felt coldly generic: "My love is with you all the time," "You're perfect for me," and the one that pissed me off the most, because year after year it just never happened: "Soon we'll be together."

H was always my *Big* secret, my life's fantastic *other option*. My escape plan. Being with H became my go-to whenever I felt low about whatever present situation I was in. Usually I was engaged in some wildly exciting adventure, or concocting one with the next barbarian or buckaroo, exciting for me, who didn't want roots, a career, family, or anything permanent. Wherever I went, whomever I was with—Hawkeye, Solstice, the faceless others—I'd end up thinking, in any unforeseen, dull moment, in between all the thrilling, endlessly annoying ones (never enough money, enough security, enough ... enoughs) I'd think then about my lifesaving escape wish:

I know I'll be with H one day. He keeps saying we're perfect for each other. I wish he wouldn't. Such nonsense just makes it harder for me to be here, right now, satisfied with what I've got.

Long before H would ask me to join him in New Zealand, while at anchor in St. Thomas, aboard my boat *Arc Isla a Isla*, I knew I desperately needed to be free from this phantom lover's grasp. He was only a teasing shadow-man, a lover who chose to never be present for *love*. Too busy, too in demand, too self-involved to meet *us* head-on with the enticements he delighted in dangling before me. Always baiting me, leading me on, sending me damn notes of "We'll be together soon." What bull caca!

I was sick of the only option H had to offer: to be his long-distance secret lover. In the years since we'd bumped into each other in Grenada, H had become a mere whisper of what he'd been to me, back then. Instead of Friedensteich Hundertwasser, as the world knew him, to me he'd become a person-less *H*, a stick-figure initial, a shadow of the famous *someone* whom I'd once adored; who, in the end, because of never fulfilling his promises, I now knew was only taking advantage of my blind affection.

Mr. Never-There for me, I mumbled whenever another of his misleading postcards arrived. H had become little more than an amorous zephyr to me, after so many rounds of his cat and mouse game.

It was a moonless night. The black glassy sea shone its inky calm all around as the Arc lay bobbing, gently, obediently at rest on her anchor in the lagoon of St. Thomas. I went up to the prow, preparing to let loose all that I'd allowed myself to fantasize about, being with H, yet always holding back, not allowing any part of myself except my imagination to join him.

Because I am—what? I asked myself. *Addicted to fantasy? Could loving the dream of this man be more intriguing to me than recognizing who H, the actual person, is? It certainly seems so.*

On the bow of my boat that pitch-dark night, I stood, breathing deeply, easily. All around, the star-brilliant sparkling night echoed my firm resolve. I was surrendering, sick of self-told lies. I was truly in the moment, and that moment was damn beautiful. For that brief moment I felt the ecstasy of being free from fear. Finally, I felt ready to let go of living this fantasy I'd fabricated.

In my hands I held two thick volumes of bound writings into which, over the years, I'd poured my heart, talking to my unreal lover all the past years, since meeting H in Grenada.

One by one, I ripped startling white pages from the thick journals, crowded with my handwriting. I crumpled each sheet and threw them quickly into the well of the sea's hungry dark maw.

The soft wind took each white paper in its grasp as it hit the black liquid flatness. Each page, a delicate miniature white swan, glided across the surface of the water. Each crumpled page a glimmering star-candle, drifting, drifting slowly away from me into the black cave of night, swallowed up, one by one, in a glowing white line. As each next page of memories landed on the flat shimmering plane of oily-looking water, the clarity of crumpled white paper contrasted sharply with the murkiness of the thick inky night.

The water's smooth ripples witnessed my unspoken vow to live in truth, from then on. I watched the ghostly fleet of migrating white paper swans, the cast-off crushed pages of needing H, fake-loving H, now recognizable as lies, my own lies. The pages' white forms slowly slithered away, floating forever into the opaque mist of Letting-Go.

Page by page, presenting shameful, rambling evidence of my self-deception—never being able, never deserving—I was now relegating these lies to their true destiny, ordering them back to where they came from—nothingness. Lies I would eliminate, not myself.

I cast off my copious outpourings to H that I'd never sent him. He, too famous, too old, too self-centered, too committed to not-being-committed, too damn far away, always moving, always distracted, he who would tantalize me again and again with his "We'll soon be together…"

I didn't rush.

There were so many pages. A luminous long line of white paper floated away on the black water. It unfurled as if I was shedding this snake's skin that had wound so tightly round my heart, strangling me for too long.

I didn't read anything on the sheets, not a word. They were meant for him, not me. I felt a pang of awakening achievement, watching the glowing, outcast epistles float away in the dead of night. By this act I was now choosing Self Love. There were no more excuses for pain. I was tossing out the illusion of love, ready to find the real deal, at last. The tiny swans drifted away into the moonless blackness, pure white symbols of my breaking the chains of *being in* love with—nothing—not even a dream.

My heart rattled awake. A sense of vitality shook me. The ability to accept life for what it is, was mine again.

With this literary burial at sea, I cast out the alluring addiction I had to un-realness. My reality from then on, was to try to *be* love. In time, I would learn to love myself, first and foremost. I knew then, that this is what I had to do if I ever wanted to attract any happiness into my life.

My fantasy passion was gone. Dissolved back into the black-diamond light of the sea.

When H first sailed away from me in Grenada, he'd said the most peculiar thing I'd ever heard in my life. "I'd marry you," he said sincerely, looking me right in the eyes, "if you were a black woman." I was so shocked, so taken aback, he might as well have said *if you were purple or tangerine colored*, the bloody hypocritical, environmental racist! As he sailed away, waving to me from the back deck, I cursed him.

After that slap in the face H gave me, there followed years of drinking and drugging myself into forgetfulness, adding to the numbing-ness I'd become so good at, ever since discovering my botanist boyfriend of three years turned out to prefer men. After H's insult, it was years before I came up for air from my cloud of wanting-to-forget.

Until … I was ready to throw those white paper swans into the darkness of oblivion.

It was then I met Hawkeye in Manhattan. Unlike H, Hawkeye insisted his way into my life. Hawkeye knew I wasn't in love with him, and really, I only wanted access to the many glassine envelopes of the White Lady that he shoveled up my nose. Hawkeye knew I was on my way back to the Caribbean from a European art-related trip, and I'd only stopped off in New York to visit a close girlfriend, at whose apartment we met.

Hawkeye knew all this about me, but all I knew about him was that he followed me back to the islands. He forced himself into my life, barged onto the shipping vessel I was hitchhiking on with two trunks that contained my entire life's possessions: art supplies and irreplaceable books in one; treasured kitchen stuff and a few clothes in the other. Hawkeye had insisted on accompanying me to Stacia where I'd been hired to do months' worth of murals at a fancy resort.

Which turned out to be a lie. There was no resort. Only a strip of obscenely barren concrete motel rooms on a lonely windward beach the new owner hadn't been clearly told about, when he'd purchased his *resort* sight unseen back in New York. Hawkeye was there to comfort me getting bamboozled, again. Hawkeye thumped his chest and roared at the sea, at the full moon above, proclaiming his love, his need for me. I was honest; I told him I felt nothing. I was numb. I only wanted his *white lady*. Then—around our non-stop coke-talk yap sessions, our relationship, one-sided platonic for me, hangdog puppy-horny for him—Hawkeye told me about Yuko.

Who? I said, suddenly alert, dead real in a fog of wanting-to-forget coke buzz.

Hawkeye told me Yuko was the Japanese woman he'd met when he played pro-ball in Venice, Italy.

"What's that?" I asked. "You say she'd been divorced from some famous Viennese artist?"

He told me Yuko was crazy about him but he didn't feel the same about her, the opposite of how Hawkeye wanted to be with me. "We were just friends, Yuko and me, on my end," he said. But Yuko kept insisting herself into his life, so Hawkeye had to keep telling her, "No, I don't feel like that."

My eyes opened widely. The fog of forgetfulness was lifting, momentarily.

In a few short questions, of course I found out Yuko was "the Japanese artist wife" that my H had been married to for several years, with whom he'd lived all over Europe, Oceania, and Japan; with whom he'd learned about composting humus toilets, commonly found in the Japanese countryside, and learned about the masterful reproductions that Japanese are so renowned for. Yuko was the ex-wife of the phantom my life had been entangled with for far too long, even then.

Hawkeye insisted he loved me. "Look, it's fate," he said, trying to convince me to love him back. "Your H, my Yuko. You and me, it's meant to be, can't you see? How close our degrees of separation really are?"

I kept saying, "No, I don't feel like that about you."

Then we'd do a few more lines of the lady.

Our attraction was repeating the same pattern he'd gone through with H's ex, only Hawkeye and I had reversed the roles he'd played with Yuko.

Meanwhile, my life had crumbled to ashes, once again. After barging into my life, insisting on accompanying me to St. Eustatius, comforting me with excessive lines of coke, after realizing I'd been duped by a fake-mural job, after having spent the last of my money to get myself and all my belongings there. We did more lines, realizing how eerily we were connected through our respective, spooky relationships with Yuko and H. I was confounded beyond measure.

Both of us not being able to love those who claimed to love us. Or something like that.

Hawkeye insisted I marry him. He wanted to take me away from the mess I'd made of things. There was no resort, only an abandoned goat shed with no roof. I'd been duped by a New York con man. I had to make up my mind. Either leave everything I owned behind, literally, and find a boat to hop aboard and take me to the other side of the world (next on my list of escape possibilities) or—marry Hawkeye and let him take care of this mess I'd made of my life. Even though I didn't love him, he was nice enough. Intelligent. Generous with his coke. He talked about things I liked: we read the same books, we liked the idea that we were both spiritual, even though we really didn't know what that meant.

I was too high on the coke he'd brought, then had more Fed-Exed to him, to decide. I tossed my three coins and sought the answer in my faithful sidekick I took everywhere, a beat-up copy of the *I Ching*, the *Book of Change*. The hexagram I received was vague, as they always were. The changing line could have pointed this way or that, depending on how you looked at it, regarding the situation of marrying I asked about. My disturbed mind as open as a tomb, I interpreted the oracle I received that desperate day— Preponderance of the Great—as *It's Great Good Fortune to take action*. So all right, I told Hawkeye, Yes, I will marry you. Even though I honestly didn't know what the book, the oracle was trying to tell me, and I certainly didn't know what else to do.

In retrospect, of course I had to go with Hawkeye. I had to plunge headfirst into the life of a true, free-flowing addict, which his pro-ball contracts allowed me, encouraged me, afforded me to do. Together we returned to his lovely house in Herzliya, Israel, where we lived for the next year as two wino-cokeheads, pot, hash, and any other kind of anything-goes type druggies. By the time we left to return to the States, I was sick, my liver nearly gone from bad Israeli wine. I was at the end of my tether. Still, I couldn't stop using. Even though I wanted to. Unlike Hawkeye who would sadly die an alcoholic, decades later, I wanted out of this living hell.

Back in the States, in a lousy New Jersey rental on the other side of the George Washington Bridge, with nothing in the refrigerator except beer, thinking about sticking my head in the oven and doing a Sylvia Plath, I was saved by a phone call from my sister. Who reminded me I had a choice: I could leave. That was how I got the courage to change. My sister's phone call—received as I paced the kitchen floor, staring at the oven door which was wide open and ready for me to gas up—saved me. I fled Hawkeye right after my sister's face-slapping words. My addiction to Low was about to come to an end.

Without Hawkeye, I might have continued being just an iffy kind of fuck up, someone who wasn't stupid enough to take the serious, deadly plunge into non-stop chemically altering my reality. I have a huge degree of appreciation for Hawkeye, having rescued me from one kind of mess, and bringing me to the final end of my slowly unraveling rope. No longer was I anchored anywhere, after we came together. Hawkeye waltzed me to my bottom. Without him, I might never have crashed and burned, and been able to rise up out of the ashes of my totaled heap of bones to be the person I am today.

Someone whom I came, in time, to quite like.

CHAPTER 7

suspended in expectation

A s the twilight pewter sneaks in before dawn, we hear the soothing crow of Roostie reminding us that another new day is soon upon us. Always, that sound brings a satisfying recognition that might be called joy. Then there's anticipation too, with knowing that Roostie's job is being done, awakening us all. His sound echoes in waves pure and bright, like the new day itself.

Even before the Blue Person, that *inner lover* who'd become awakened inside of me, I had known intuitively that I had to change. The type of obsessive take-no-survivors rampage I had been on was killing me! This so-called "love" addiction I'd had went hand-in-hand with loving to get high, loving thrills, and the ever more dangerous one of loving to change partners. With AIDS so rampant then, I wasn't stupid. Years later, I would find myself barely missing the bullet when I found out one of my earliest boyfriends, the botanist, had died of the virus. I knew drugs and drinking would slowly kill me, but the virus was way more lethal. Already, my organs had started shutting down from my extreme excesses in Israel, thanks to Hawkeye's fat bank account and habit, as equally insatiable as mine. The taste of bile from my damaged liver was often in my mouth. My face had become alcohol-swollen while my torso remained drug-skinny—and hell, I was only in my early thirties!

Finally, I crashed.

It happened right after I'd run away from my complicated life in New York City, where I was living after fleeing Hawkeye, and wound up in that D.R. jail, after one-last-fling, an extravaganza of self-forgetting. After that plane ride back home, when Dad told me his long-held secret, asking for my forgiveness for being a lousy father. I guess I needed to have one last binge, because right after (upon being released from the emergency room I was rushed to) that's when I managed to pick myself up. That's what it took for me to decide I wanted to live, not die.

Dragging my sorry ass to "the Program" … I asked for help. And I got it. Little by little, I got better. I learned how to live without booze, drugs, drama, and the never-ending toxic relationships and overkill drama that goes along with destructive addictions. Along with renewing my organs and feeling the ache leave my kidneys, hoping I'd managed to save my wretchedly overdone gallbladder as my liver detoxed, my lungs emptying from the yellow junk that'd filled them from my now-departed nicotine habit—I slowly changed. Body, mind, and spirit: all of me, started to heal. I began to look in the mirror without cringing. The incessant chirping in my mind, quieted. Gradually, I became calmer. Slowly, I accepted the miracle of being given another chance without breaking down in tears of remorse, or freezing in fear of "I can't do this!"

As I slowly got better, a new kind of art emerged from my not-so-frozen heart, my less frenzied mind, my unshaking hand, now that I was being freed, bit by bit, from the previous chains of my warped perceptions. Light came now, in through new openings, tiny cracks that penetrated my clouded mind, revealing a new way for me. They watched—from a distance—because I was not yet aware of their presence, these invisible Unseen helpers all of us have. I'd heard, but I hadn't yet believed that all we have to do is ask for help. Then, the spiritual energy that's available to any of us, is able to be received. Everything from this point on, I kept promising my mirror, would be different.

The fancifully skewed, cacophonous stuff I'd been calling *my work*—I dragged that maudlin, morbid, overly-serious dark stuff I called "art" to the dump one fine day. It was the second year of my getting-sober adventure. In secret delight I hid behind a wrecked refrigerator carcass, thrilled to be watching as human scavengers flocked around the stack of perplexing, yet what had been to me, intoxicating paintings. I left them in the to-be-recycled area, a gaily striped, circus tent affair at the oh-so-hip East Hampton dump.

Peering out from behind my hiding place, I smiled seeing those old works of mine—too awful to bother being sentimental over—being hauled off by hoarders, junk dealers, bad-taste aficionados: the lower echelons of this town I was living in, a summer favorite of the fashionably rich and famous. It felt like only seconds, after dropping my carload of angsty old paintings I'd lugged there, that they were scattered, dragged away by a flock of pack-rats who raced away in raggedy old Mercedes and Volvos, a rickety Peugeot, a rusty Citroën. As I watched in secret delight, imagining my cryptic works hanging crookedly in doublewide trailers, over blaring TVs, with Jeopardy or Wheel of Fortune turned on way too loud—I laughed, feeling free, absolutely re-born!

I had no regrets letting go of those past efforts, big and small pieces, some with odd additions sewed or patched, painted with oils, acrylics, or alkyds mixed with spit, blood, and sweat. Great relief washed over my newly transformed sober self. These relics, ritual-izing a past homage to being a damaged person, were now, finally, gone for good. My old body of work, years' worth, now dispersed to the winds of fate. Out of my sight forever.

Back at my cleared-out studio home in the woodsy part of East Hampton, I resumed work on my latest piece, a human-sized wooden screen depicting the feminine creative energy on one side, the masculine aggressive energy on the other. Both sides shared a cut-out hole, an oval I'd sawed in the wood panel, head-high, in which I suspended a large clear crystal, inserted with a copper mount. It was meant to represent both sides' shared head. I stood back and studied the nearly finished piece, pleased with my commitment to documenting this new inner journey I was on, by making such completely different art. I chuckled, thinking of all my old works, gone for good, save for the well-lit photos I always took of them. *Good riddance*, I whispered. *Now I'm free to make* creations of everything I've always wanted to become: trapeze artist, sky and deep blue sea diver, spirit-dancer, Light-chaser extraordin-aire.

Standing close to the colorful screen, I closed my eyes. I saw the hazy silhouette of my imagined, perfect mate standing next to me, and—freaky, this—I sensed some little kids were there, alongside me, waiting for me. Me, who'd never thought much about children ever before. I smiled and thought, *Yes, we'll adopt, as soon as we find each other*. I wondered, *Where is he? Is he near, or far from me right now?*

From that very day I cast my old work aside at the East Hampton dump, my new work began to glow, reflecting the same inner Light I felt and saw everywhere. It'd always been there, I'd just never believed, or chose to see the Light, the positive side. Now, my art became a way to consciously reach out to others. It was infused with this newfound sense I had, that humanity, and life itself, really wasn't out to do me in. My hands created pieces that vibrated from the intention I placed within them, hidden among images, felt in my materials. Pleased with the vicissitudes and structure of each new work that rushed out of my creative fountain, my once rusted-over heart was pried open.

The first day of spring arrived with me musing over how to create the future I'd envisioned with each new day. First my art changed; now I was ready to change the rest of my life.

Ahhh, the human heart: the only reliable barometer of a person's Truth. The Sign of Signs that beats away rhythmically, pulsing Love in the blood, through our veins.

My heart yearned to know what Love really was, now that I'd turned away from its dysfunctional cousins. My entire body tingled with excitement, wondering in what shape, form, and personage this new and pure kind of Love would arrive in.

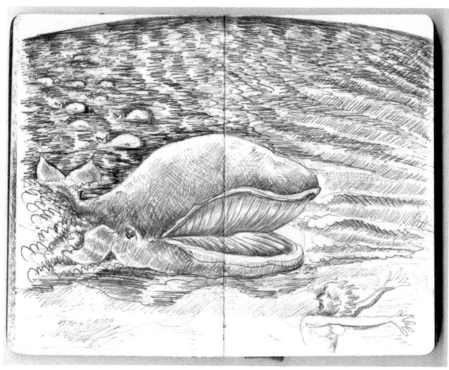

the Unseens ... can hear the painful cry of the ocean's giants

CHAPTER 8

the alchemy of love

*S*ilent-to-humans, the sound of the whale's piercing sonar reached our guides on the other side. Hearing the cry of the almost-extinct whales, the Unseens, these body-less souls, spirits, energy sources, whatever you want to call them—they can hear the painful cry of the ocean's giants. The whale sings so mournfully, knowing that its species is almost gone from the face of the Earth, like so many other species before. Some species, of course, have evolved to become something more sustainable: the process of natural selection. Evolution's sacrifices upon the altar of attaining a higher good. Changes made by, and in Nature's pursuit of progress.

The whale, the great watery mammalian mountain of flesh and bone, and some of its closely related cetaceans, including many species of porpoises, are clearly innocent victims of humankind's sloppy stewardship. Unconcerned (and incompetent) humans came before our present generation with their mistakes throwing off the balance of Earth's atmosphere, its waters, its resources. It's our duty to rectify their mistakes.

The Unseens know, as we hybrid vigors do, the great peril our world is in.

The building-sized whale swims, but many have stopped breeding. Why? North Atlantic giants suffer from the continuous search for offshore oil deposits, the use of seismic air gun and sonar testing, constant blasts every 10 seconds, 24/7, creating such stress to the already endangered leviathans, that biologists say they can't engage in the leisure of mating due to being subjected to such states of unease.

Some people stop thinking about mating too, when they're over-stressed; others think about nothing besides sex at stressful times. All animals stop normal functioning when they're over-burdened. In reaction to stress—all of us animals naturally change.

The whales are changing by disappearing.

We humans? We are changing in various ways in response to the many stressors of modern life. Some of us have forgotten to take care of ourselves, denying the most important thing about our human existence, our spiritual nature.

Stressful times make people withdraw.

No wonder many of us have forgotten to take care of others, forsaken not only protecting whales but other humans in distress. We must protect all creatures, so we can live harmoniously, together, in our beautiful garden Earth-home.

How did such hardships like pollution and human conflict take over from the joy of simply being alive? It doesn't have to be so. Learning to accept that change is happening, organically—as it always has—is part of *accepting the way things are*. Helping others to unravel the challenge that has ensnared us is our sacred duty. Resistance to change traps so many modern-day folks. People need to question, and find answers, themselves. Change is good. It's just damn uncomfortable when we can't see the light at the end of the long dark transition-trench we find ourselves in, as change is occurring. For now, yes, we're right in the middle of evolution's current, swept into its dark passages and dangerous currents. A better time lays just ahead, for us as well as for future generations, if we can only foster the Light, and detach from the influence of darkness all around us.

These are stressful times, but we HVs believe there is always hope. Always!

After the West Indies I traveled with Hawkeye to the Middle East and ended up discovering, first-hand, just why so many of our kind, humankind, love to hate. Spending an entire year living close to Tel Aviv, I set up an art studio in my home, and searched for answers in a place where so much of the world's great stressors originated and still today, remains.

The official Jewish nation, Israel was created by the U.N. in my birth-year 1947, when India also became freed from British sovereignty. Because of that I felt an odd affinity for both countries' pains and sufferings. Israel's people, Hebrews and Palestinians, keep trying to forge a life together after the Jewish diaspora, resulting from millennia-old conflict and hatred. As the only Shiksa (female non-Jew, in Yiddish) in Hawkeye's and my close circle of neighbors and friends, I was called upon to light many of the religious ones' stoves, a task forbidden to practicing Jews on the Shabbat.

All day Friday is the holiest day of the week for practicing Muslims, of which there are many in Israel observing this day of religious remembrance. From Friday at dusk until Saturday's sunset is the Jewish Shabbat. For Christians, their holy day, the Sabbath, of honoring God by worship and with no work, is Sunday. Jerusalem, the center of all three Abrahamic religions—Judaism, Christianity, Islam—is a city of spiritual observance for all three. Therefore, three full days of the week, from Friday through Sunday, are religious days. Nowhere else on the face of the Earth are all three religions given equal respect. This sacred city is less than an hour's drive from Tel Aviv, where I lived in the affluent burb of Herzliya Pituach with Hawkeye, my Jewish-American athlete-husband at the time.

One day, after talking with a gray haired, friendly neighborhood Jewish grandmother in Herzliya, who always greeted me "My favorite Shiksa!" I began to understand how the most longstanding and solemn rip in the interwoven human story has such a clear and obvious solution, to me at least.

One day over tea I, in my thirties at the time, asked the kind-hearted elder before me, "How do you *really* feel about your Arab neighbors, Rivka?"

By *neighbors* I meant not just the courageous Palestinians who had remained in their century's old homeland, now called Israel since the U.N. designated Palestine to the Jews at the conclusion of World War II. I wondered aloud to Rivka how so many Jews had come to live there, in Israel, so filled with conflict as it was since its inception. Jews, of course, had been wandering the Earth in a wide diaspora for generation upon generation for thousands of years, long before Palestine was ever formed. The question I posed to Rivka referred to not just the displaced Palestinians who'd decided to stay, or leave, after the Jews arrived back by the droves to their spiritual homeland of Israel—but to all Semites, which includes all descendants of Abraham, by blood or religious allegiance. This includes people who are not blood related to Arabs or Jews, but who define themselves by their choice of religion, the converts. I personally know non-Islamic Arabs who range from secular atheists to Syrian Orthodox Christians, for instance, and Palestinians who are Baha'is, an all-inclusive religion. Some of my Jewish friends have no special beliefs other than being smart and successful. When asked what religion they were, a famous Jewish writer's father once responded, "We're Americans."

In return for asking her my simple question, I got from Rivka an easily understood reason for why the entire world is still reckoning, to this very day, with her ancestors' pivotal grudge. In a whispered voice shaking with strong emotion, my usually con-siderate neighbor tried to honestly answer my question in the bosom of her sunny kitchen. I was shocked to see Rivka's upper lip curl inward as she thought of her answer. Such a look of visceral anger I'd seen before, but only when talking to victims of abuse, war, or other atrocities.

"I know how the unfixable break between us Jews and Arabs began," my Herzliya neighbor sighed. Moments before, her lips had arced upward in a gentle smile, but now—upon answering my question—they transformed into a harsh resolute line of ugly anger. I noted her chin quivering uncontrollably. I sat motionless, afraid I had upset this gentle woman. I never would have guessed the dire, disturbing consequences of my curiosity, or I would never have asked.

"Our common hatred," Rivka said, "began with the meanness and jealousy between two women thousands of years ago, Sarah and Hagar. Sarah was the ninety-year-old wife of Abraham, much too old for childbirth. She was a pious Hebrew woman, who, the Torah says, willingly gave her Egyptian slave, Hagar, to Abraham as a second wife. Sarah sacrificed her position as head wife so the younger woman could produce an heir for the old man. Abraham's first-born son from Hagar was named Ishmael. Sarah gladly did this favor for her husband, the Book says. Abraham and Sarah both knew an heir was needed. It was *her* idea, not Abraham's, so that he, the greatest of the ancient Jews, would give his people a new leader. Only after Ishmael was born first, did Sarah amaze everyone when the old woman miraculously became pregnant, and gave birth to Abraham's second son, Isaac.

"The story turned bad here," Rivka continued, "revealing the intense jealously Sarah felt upon the birth of Hagar's son who, of course, was half-Egyptian. As soon as her own healthy, miracle-son was born, Sarah started demanding Abraham to kick Hagar and Ishmael out of the family compound. At first, Abraham resisted. Sarah's unrelenting arguments finally won sway.

"Abraham gave in, banishing Hagar and Ishmael, forcing them to flee back to her own country." Rivka grew more excited now. "In Egypt, the clan of Hagar's son became known as the Ishmaelites. History tells us the Ishmaelites were among the earliest of people to be called Arabs, because Egypt was part of the vast ancient empire known as Arabia."

Here Rivka took a deep breath. She sat nodding her head, as if she could hear her own mother and grandmother recounting the same story for her as a young girl. Again, she spoke.

"I'm sorry to say," Rivka's tone went very low, "that the hateful rivalry between our two clans of Abraham's descendants started with Sarah's jealous rage against Hagar. It's as plain to see as reading scripture. All our problems started with those two women; an ancient Jewish woman hating an ancient Egyptian woman." Rivka's upper lip curled more tightly inward, baring her teeth as she spoke the next words. "Naturally, my own feelings arose from my ancestor's, Sarah's. I know that. But I can't help it. It's in my blood. Hate breeds hate."

I sat staring into Rivka's transformed face, shocked at the now deformed, shriveled old woman I saw. A once lovely face had become pure ugliness. Her features reflected her inbred revenge, envy, and every other poisonous negative emotion that punishes a person's features. My formerly pleasant looking neighbor had shape-shifted in front of me into an unbelievably repulsive crone. I was shocked numb. When she gushed her next statement, I caught myself gasping, uncomfortably needing fresh air.

"I can't help it," Rivka repeated in a pitiful moan. "I wish it weren't true. I wish I could forgive them. I feel the hatred poisoning my veins. We Jews have always hated the Arabs, and they hate us, too. It feels like there's nothing we can do about it. Hating each other has been our custom for so long now, we simply don't know any other way. I'm sorry, but it's true."

Mumbling my apologies, I exited as quickly as I could from Rivka's kitchen, needing different air to breathe. I was suddenly afraid of the old lady who, for many previous afternoons, had shared numerous cups of tea with me. Together, before this, we'd laughed at humorous stories from her treasure chest of memories without a single trace of rancor on her part. After her freely shared unguardedness, whenever I think back to that day, I thank Rivka for having been so honest, in revealing her deep-seated hatred of Arabs for me to understand better. In the age-old test of human memory, hatred seems to always outrank love as easiest to remember. Evil, fierce aggression, and violence emotionally scar us. The wounds of resentment go much deeper, more impressionably than compass-sionate, peaceful interactions, of which, surely, there must have been some between Arabs and Jews in centuries past, just as there are many today.

The same can be said of our own personal memories. Hardships outrank good times when it comes to easiest-to-recall. People tend to not forget acts of unfair or oppressive use of power, whether done to us personally (especially in childhood) or cruel government acts that lead up to violence and bloodshed, as in the current global refugee crisis. Never again would I be able to remember Rivka as the dear generous soul who lived next door to me, in whose bright ochre kitchen I'd learned to make so many delicious Jewish dishes, her matzos, latkes, and gnocchis. Instead, her words became seared into my memory as one of life's messengers of raw Truth. She was the person who'd caused me to realize it was two ancient women who initiated this sorrowful rent in the woven fabric of our human family that sadly, the world still suffers from today.

The anachronistic conflict between Jews and Arabs represents the main cause of stress in our international culture. The solution to this ancient animosity must be resolved. Along with the critical environmental crisis our planet and species face, it is the most crucial challenge that prevents other global efforts from being realized, because of the continued, paralyzing fear of terrorist threats it causes everywhere on the globe.

Conflicts between groups of people is synonymous to saving Earth's atmosphere. Both issues are fueled by fear and can be remedied by elevating the consciousness of humankind. By addressing climate change, facing the unprecedented number of dying species our world is losing today, the whales, bees, frogs and numerous others, and ending age-old conflicts such as the Arab-Israel one, our blended family realizes—and heals, the primary cause of our worldwide blended family's breakdown—the disconnect that happened from our natural state of wonder. In healing, we regain our ability to accept one another as sparks of divinity. By healing the rift originating from the conflict arising from these two ancient women's quarrel, by talking about it, discussing our need to heal it—our world *is healing*, and returning to our Nature-based wholesomeness.

When people understand this important fact—the need to return to revering Nature as we did earlier in human history—they will also understand why nurturing-leadership (female and male leaders who *own*, and work with their feminine-spiritual aspect, the more open and accepting side of our common human nature) can heal our broken world. The world needs the compassionate, loving, spiritual-nurturing kind of leadership that feminine energy has, in contrast to the more aggressive, materialistic, competitive stance of masculine energy we've been beholden to, since Nature lost her stance as our planet's deity.

By deity, I mean *practical, everyday center* of our society's focus; not an image to bow to, or iconic totem to be worshipped with sacrifice, rituals, or exclusion of other beliefs. Nature must be respected as the *essence of our Being*, is what I mean by returning Nature to the center of importance *It* needs to be, in order for a healthy, balanced world to proceed into the future.

Just as a balanced person utilizes both their masculine and feminine energies at appropriate times, so too, our blended family of humankind needs to correct its conquest-orientation, hungry materialism attributed to more masculine attributes than the spiritualized, Nature-oriented feminine ones. Only with nurturing, insightful leaders can our world's various groups heal this antediluvian schism begun by the thousands-years-old quarrel between Sarah and Hagar.

Love alone has the power to heal misunderstandings. Acceptance of others is a characteristic worthy of cultivating in all hearts and cultures. Until we heal, starting with one person at a time—and function as One Blended Family of Humankind—our entire world will remain sick, toxic, and stressed to the max.

What I've just proclaimed may come as a surprise to the shouting angry people who blame all of modern-day woes on misogynistic male superiority and paternalistic power. Listen to Rivka's recounting with open hearts and minds. Only women (or men who acknowledge their spiritual, feminine side as well as their masculine nature, both equally) have this natural nurturing power to create the healing environment that can resolve the ancient rip in our human family's interwoven web.

Women caused the breakdown; women have to fix it.

Once we realize this and allow spiritually aware leaders—male or female or in-between leaders—to nurture us back to health, our full attention can be directed to solving other urgent challenges that threaten our world's vulnerability. Pollution can be solved by clean energy; animal endangerment as well as devastating human conflict can be solved by compassionate, conscious choices. The world needs to be loved and cared for. But first—each of us must heal ourselves. Healing our old wounds will provide new, mitigating solutions to the world's critical needs, such as globally replacing fossil fuels, and discovering a cure for cancer and other deadly diseases. A spiritual approach to life reverses the addiction to self-destructive tendencies so prevalent among humankind.

Women are now more involved in leading others in all walks of life: economic, industrial, scientific, political, spiritual, ad infinitum. There is a new goddess for this time of the Divine Female energy arising to reverse all of humankind's current troubles. She is *Civitas*, the contemporary deity (created by sculptor Audrey Flack at the end of the twentieth century). Civitas represents awakened spirituality, the awakened consciousness of this time we're in, individually, and as a united species. We are now discovering the unlimited heights of our human capabilities, so we can heal and make whole, what has been broken. Four thirty-foot bronze statues of Civitas (located at an intersection in Rock Hill, South Carolina) show her holding up iconic symbols depicting how this modern goddess nourishes, guides, protects and inspires all of humankind.

The epoch we are currently in, according to the ancient Vedic scriptures, is nothing less than the one in which humankind attains its true state, that of our *Divine Nature*. Likewise, Christians say this is the era of the *awakened Christ Consciousness*. Buddhists say this time now, is the birth of the *New Buddha Consciousness*. Those reading this book know you're already awakened, otherwise you wouldn't be attracted to it. However the spiritual awakening of humankind is expressed, our species' ability to access higher states of consciousness is happening already. Right here and now.

Exercising my creative right to delve into new uplifting ideas, my chosen art form, I'm happily calling this new kind of spiritualized human—straight men and women, LGBTQ, gender neutrals, fluids, in-betweens of all sorts, anyone in touch with both their masculine and female nature simultaneously, people who balance their inner power with their outer capabilities—every single person, young or old, folks who are capable of solving our world's seemingly unsolvable challenges: this is the *hybrid vigor* person.

Ever since Rivka told me her sad hateful story, it's been my firm belief that women of the here and now and in the near future, are the living embodiment of Civitas. We are the ones, we hybrid vigors, who will bring unity and healing to all. Super-women, super-men, and super-thems, too, each and every one of us capable of nurturing, healing this wound with Love, making us wholly human again. We HVs will mend this rip, and any others that fester deep within our collective human family. The state of accepting each other is key to forgiving. Spiritual leadership is needed to bring us into balance, a state in which we, as a blended human family, will continue to thrive and prosper with Love as our commonality, not suspicion, judgment, competition, or hatred.

The diaspora throughout the then-known world of the ancient oppressed Hebrews, began centuries before Jesus was born amongst them. The migration of Jewish refugees continued in even greater earnest after the fall of Jerusalem to the Roman army in 70 CE. The Mediterranean region formerly known as Canaan, would from then on be known as Palestine, inhabited predominantly by Islamic Arabs. Until, that is, Israel was created by the U.N., when the Jewish people's ancient homeland was given back to them in the aftermath of WWII.

Judaism as well as Christianity and Islam, all claim Abraham as their paterfamilias. These three world religions are rooted in the same Semitic blood relations. All three religious groups and their variously mixed, blended descendants, are Abraham's distant, but direct progeny, if not by blood, by faith.

When I discovered this fact, which was reinforced after my year-long stay in Israel, I became convinced that every Jewish, Christian, and Muslim person is, in fact, a true cousin of each other; because we all originate, whether by blood, adoption, or by conversion, from the same blended family as Sarah's and Hagar's. Jews and Arabs who share blood ancestry, share the same hereditary traits and DNA, as they do with descendants of the earliest Christians, who, like Jesus himself, were Jewish. Everyone knows how romantic love has no racist, cultural, or religious barriers. My father's Pilgrim ancestors of Plymouth rock, Massachusetts, notoriously mated with the local Native American indigenous: hence my super prominent cheekbones.

I found it increasingly incongruous, the longer I stayed in Israel, to learn how deeply these two cultures, Jewish and Arabic, remain steeped in such hateful intolerances as they insist on perpetuating.

How very sad, that their apparently uncontrollable, unconscious prejudices as Rivka so honestly revealed to me, continue to burn, unconsciously, in too many hearts today—leftovers from a four-millennia-old rivalry ignited by two well-meaning but bitchy women. Fighting over which of them had the right to bear an heir to the great religious and ethnic leader of their times.

Sarah's son Isaac would go on to marry Rebecca. One of their sons, Abraham's grandson, was named Jacob, who remained in Canaan, later to be called Palestine. Jacob would be renamed *Israel* (meaning, "a man seeing God") when he found himself one day wrestling with an angel, according to the biblical parable. The origin of Israel, the country's name itself, you see, was influenced by the interaction of Unseen forces. Likewise, many events in human history have, and will continue to be, influenced by powers not easily understood by logical, rational, *show-me-the-proof* human cognition preferred by people not yet comfortable with tapping, and comfortably using, their higher faculties: their expanded consciousness that goes beyond logic and rational thought.

When I heard Rivka's confession of her culture's ingrained hatred for *all Arabs*, I sensed then, that the world would one day have to be transformed into a better variety of human being—by modern women's involvement. From the moment she revealed her uncontrollable loathing, I knew that only awakened humans, those of us who break free of being chained to tradition, and even logic, people who honor their feminine-spiritual natures—could heal the ancient wounding caused by the two bickering women of Abraham's Real Housewives of Long-ago.

Soon after Ishmael and Hagar were banished from Canaan, but before the Unseen angel wrestled with Jacob, God came to Abraham and ordered him, as a test of his faith, to sacrifice Isaac, Sarah's and his only son. Only at the very last moment, with the knife raised high to strike did God, the King of the Unseens Himself, stop Abraham from murdering his beloved son and official heir, Isaac. Father Abraham's knife-strike halted mid-air upon hearing God's intervention, "Stop!" Then Abraham noticed a bleating ram caught in a nearby brambly bush, and, obeying the Unseen Voice, released his son and finished the demanded sacrifice with the poor trapped animal. No one who reads and sincerely relates to the significance of biblical stories, asks if God is "good" or "bad" because He takes such actions that, if done by a mere human, would surely be judged as "wrong," or even "insane."

◎

We twenty-first century people, guided by our feminine-side, the spiritual inner Self each person possesses (the masculine-side is defined as having more materialistic, divide-and-conquer, separate-from or scoffing-of Divine attributes)—whatever gender a person is, or wishes to claim—we can all spiritualize ourselves. We hybrid vigors are already being midwives for others joining our new subspecies of humankind that is currently healing our world.

The healing happens one *awakened* person at a time. I became convinced of this that long-ago day, in Rivka's cumin-and-cardamom flavored kitchen. That the vanguard of heart-opened souls—females and males who are nurturers, not conquerors—these are the individuals who are igniting the ceremonial fires of human transformation. As soon as I acknowledged the necessity for Earth's healing, I began to notice how quickly this tribe of healers, my own tribe now, are stitching up Sarah and Hagar's formerly irreparable rupture.

This shift toward higher consciousness is already in full swing. In the late twentieth century, this pivotal point in human history, our spiritual awakening, was celebrated worldwide by people who gathered in sacred circles. Prophesied by several diverse sources, including the Mayan calendar and the Bible's Book of Revelations, the number of awakened souls—144,000, to be precise, awakened *sun dancers* (as organizers referred to the participating *awakened people*)—had been reached at this time. That number of transformed humans was the tipping point, creating an ensuing domino-effect that assures, in essence, the inevitability of humankind's global, spiritual transformation, in entirety. By sheer force of this millennia-ago, exact, predicted number, the spiritualization of humankind was declared to be then underway, and unstoppable. Talk about a grassroots revolution! Nothing now will ever stop the spread of minds-being-ignited by others' enlightened minds! Enlightenment, you see, is catching. Human consciousness already reached, thirty years back, the point of no return on its journey to becoming the new subspecies of hybrid vigors.

Every year, every month, every minute since then—more enlightened Earth-healers are committing to help mend our broken world—our damaged atmosphere, our fractured, divisive Big Heart of humanity. There's no stopping us. We are already more humanly whole than we've ever been, since a few of our ancestors started walking upright and away from the rest of their tribe of apes.

After that afternoon in Herzliya, Israel, I started to ask myself, "How am I supposed to stop self-loathing and start ...? Loving myself? How on earth shall I begin?" I wondered.

Childhood wounds go deep, a Voice whispered in my ear. *Healing begins with self-forgiveness. You've already started because you're able to recognize the need to change. Now, learn to love your Self, your better part, not that old part that no longer serves you. Everything starts with awareness of the Self. This Self is the pure, natural part of you; it's connected by invisible energy to all Seens and Unseens. Love, and accept all parts of your Self first. Calm your inner demons, and they'll disappear. The best place to start is within your own heart and mind. Start with what is right in front of you ... and decide to make your life ... right now! ... a prayer.*

I was ready. And so, a teacher magically, instantly appeared.

From this noted meditation master, I learned that patience and forgiveness are prerequisite to developing any inner strengths. Anyone desiring to change the dross of Hatred into the alchemical gold of Love better have plenty of both forgiveness and patience.

Trouble was, patience was never one of my virtues.

The great paradox, known by all who wish to not be so fucked up as we once were, is that in order to have patience, a requirement of the spiritual path, one has to learn how to develop it. Catch-22.

My degree of fucked-up-ness was so immense, requiring so much patience to change, that I quickly had to get some—or I knew I'd die. My anger, my blaming others, was so out of whack, I knew I'd never make it, never get better, if I didn't re-program myself, and quickly. Thinking about others' instead of my own needs didn't come intuitively to me.

In order to nurture myself, I trusted my teacher's expert guidance. I learned to accept what *Is* and what *Was*, starting with one painful memory at a time. Soon enough, I got so good at accepting *What Is* that, with just a few breaths' worth of letting-go, having practiced tuning into Spirit (through meditation) quite a bit, I grew to accept anything as it unfolded before me. Things that I had never been able to let go of, got washed out of my disturbed psyche by using the best tool of detachment, that of steady prayer. The great holy word of "Help!" became my favorite in the early years of eradicating those inner demons of mine.

Patience taught me many things. I learned to create boundaries instead of wasting my limited life-energy by giving it away. I learned how to distance myself from toxic people, places, and things. I followed the necessary, unavoidable steps to healing my Self from the damage caused by my own resentments, disrespect, and other injustices against my natural state of being whole and happy.

Forgiving someone who hurts us sounds like a banal platitude.

Yet, if I don't watch my feelings closely, even today, resentment tries to creep back into my heart. Just as it had into the heart of the otherwise loving-kind Rivka; as it had, also, into the once-friendly household relations of Hagar and Sarah. I remembered how Rivka transformed from sweet granny into bitchy old witch in two seconds flat, when she gave in to the sour poison of her old habit of cultural resentment. She, too, was a teacher of mine: of what *not to be like*. I had to remember: the only person who gets hurt by a resentment is the one who holds it. A complete, abrupt stop of spiritual growth happens when a person allows resentment of any type to poison their heart. This I had to hear whispered in my ear by my personal Unseen so many times before I got it, before I could accept it as true.

Yet for every hurtful emotional storm that hits, new growth springs forth in the healing process. Spiritual growth starts with forgiveness. If forgiveness is real, honest, and continuously worked on (not denied), one day anger and resentment just vanish. Poof! This sounds unbelievable, but I dare you to try it.

Here's how: Pray for any resentment (person, place, situation or thing) you have. Pray for *the source of your pain*, not yourself (very important!) each time the pain arises. Pray until you stop hurting inside. Give it all the time each hurt demands; as long as you need to heal the emotional bruise. If you don't, the hole inside you never heals. It just grows within you, festering like an oozing infection in your heart. Watch how asking your own Unseen for "Help!" dissolves negativities, hidden in the most secret places within our own inner selves. One day you'll notice, when you happen to think about the resentment that used to burn your guts, scream in your mind—that it's completely vanished!

"Things are not the way they appear to be," as my teacher said, was now true and real. "Because the depth of things can never be known, ever."

Patience and Acceptance, I now knew, is where Self Love

resides, right inside my own Big Heart; the same Big Heart that's connected to everyone and everything. This is also true for every other being.

This is how the darkness of destroying Hatred dissolves into luminous Love.

One out of three adults statistically suffers from anxiety or stress in one form or another. So it makes sense that forgiveness, in the form of acceptance, is a most useful *art* to cultivate. Especially if one wishes to experience more fully the feeling that life is more than just a job description, to be endured, and never heart-piercingly enjoyed, or appreciated, as the Great Gift it actually is.

I say "art" because acceptance was something I had to develop. Like learning the art of cooking, dancing, or telling jokes (darn, I never mastered that one). Or the art of happiness.

Look to the Dalai Lama as a perfect example of fostering happiness as a chosen, consistent human trait. Have you ever noticed how much he smiles and laughs? Have you ever seen how, after receiving bad news—such as another Tibetan monk immolating him- or herself, or how China continues to oppress his people—he takes an appropriate amount of time to grieve inwardly, quietly praying, and then quickly rebounds to his natural, exterior state of exuberant joy, accepting *what is*?

Yes, pain and suffering exist. To balance life, we hybrid vigors accept that life has negatives as well as positives. We quickly, resiliently, allow ourselves to heal, and, with the grace we've amassed in our "spiritual bank" can, without much to-do, bounce back from any tragedy or disappointment, no matter how devastating. Whereas many ordinary *homo sapiens* tend to cling, sorrowfully or resentfully, and far too long, to the aftereffects of crisis and tragedy. Some never can forgive. Some get locked into complaining, grieving, suffering, *choosing* to remain crippled forever—until they die. Too often, a person dies of a broken heart, literally.

Others, like myself, have had to learn *the art of acceptance*, because it didn't come natural to us, as it appears to have been to His Excellency, the fourteenth Dalai Lama. I had to choose to change, choose to develop the art of detachment. I had to practice it, get better and better at it, just as some practice the art of public speaking, twirling on ice, or *mindful* flower arranging. This new art form of mine, beginning with cultivating the two qualities of patience and acceptance, has led me to more deeply cultivate the art of Love.

Love, as everyone knows, is a phenomenon of energy. Over time, I've chosen to accept the ability to see Love everywhere I look, even in actions of others that might be called "bad" by some. I've come to realize that the worst folks and the vilest of events, play as much of a role in the drama of life as the best of things. Good or bad is now irrelevant. Everything that has occurred, had to occur, in order to lead us to this moment here, right now.

Horrific things can never be condoned. Accepting that they happen, however, is crucial for a person's release from the dis-empowering fear of being lessened by another's despicable acts. Spiritual fulfillment, therefore, is not feasible without being willing to accept that bad things *do happen*.

We don't have to like that fact, though.

Acceptance doesn't mean liking or disliking something. It just means realizing with all our mind, heart, and soul ... that *what is, Is*.

Changing something we don't like starts with choosing to change it. In order to do that, we first have to accept that what appears to be the *unacceptable* or *unchangeable* ... is happening.

Acceptance is an art form that takes some, like me, about as much time to own as a *good new* habit does, a time period comparable to comfortably playing a new instrument never touched before. Practice makes ... you know; if not perfect, practice makes new things easier to do. For some of us, we need a good long time to learn new things. For others, it can be as quickly learned as saying

"I love you" in another language.

Ich liebe dich.

Te amo.

Je t'aime.

Aš myliu tave.

CHAPTER 9

my two mothers

Roostie starts his call to awaken much earlier now. It must be hours before dawn's streaks of rosy fingers will pierce the black fabric of night. What makes him rouse us so early today? Is it because he too, senses an urgency upon the Earth? The stillness of night interrupted his own sweet rooster dreams, enough to wake him up first. Of course once he's awake, it's his obligation to awaken all within range of his dissonant, boisterous outburst. It's his job, his reason for being.

Creation made him to awaken others.

Are you listening?

I looked up at them, the two people who meant the most to me in the entire world right then.

One was Elaine, my boss; the other, Eve, my mother. They were facing each other, fiercely engaged in a battle of beliefs that sharply contrasted each another.

Each playing the role of "What *I Know* is Best!"

Eve: What she needs is insurance, health and life, and whatever other kind she can get!

Elaine: Are you kidding, Eve? Insurance for artists like us, like teZa, is anathema, a veritable death sentence.

Eve was absolutely flummoxed at this comment of Elaine's. In all her life, my mother had never been talked to in such an authoritative, abrupt, and to her, condescending manner, especially when it came to what she thought best for her *babies*, her younger one now before her.

It didn't matter to Mom that at the time her *baby* was almost forty. I would always be her baby, even as I grew closer to the age Eve was that day she and Elaine stood side by side facing me, arguing about micro-managing this fully grown, vagabond-artist woman before them, one with an equally strong will as both of theirs.

I felt as if I were watching this pair of older women debate about the true meaning of my life, played out by such unique, feisty characters, both representing a distinct part of myself which I now could more easily recognize, by observing how these two interacted together.

I was terribly amused more than anything. So I kept quiet and observing, my favored, most reliable method of interacting with others.

Elaine de Kooning was my art mentor and spiritual mother, the supporter and champion I'd always craved, but never had in my own overly critical mom. Eve and Elaine were born in the same year, 1918. Both were in their sixties then, yet right there their similarities ended. Other than they were both white American women.

They could have been in the same school class, but they'd never have hung out in the same gang. Eve was a first generation, all-practical, no nonsense hard-working immigrant farm girl. Menial jobs, the first in a factory, were her reward for having quit high school because she didn't have *proper shoes* to wear. Getting dressed up in a skirt and not-silk stockings, earning enough, though, to walk around in good leather pumps, in those hardscrabble pre-World War II days—gave her, my working-class mom, the self-esteem she'd never found in her two years of high school. English was her second language, picked up quickly when she started to walk the three miles from her family's rural farm to the one-room schoolhouse on the outskirts of town. Mom was smart enough to pick up bookish skills to mask her latent feelings of inferiority, being a daughter of dirt-rich, money-poor truck farmers.

Ironically, during the Depression it was to Eve's family's farm that hungry folks in the area, or just passing through, flocked to. Time after time strangers, mostly men on the move searching for work, would end up sitting in my Grammom's cozy farm kitchen, saying, "Yes'm" when she, Antonina, asked in garbled English, if he'd care for one more fried egg—and then another. Mom told us funny, poignant stories of the many men who'd eat more than a dozen freshly laid eggs apiece, in one sitting, fried up one by one by Antonina, until they'd had their fill.

Such were the rewards—good healthy food and lots of it—of being a tiller of the earth during hard times.

Elaine wasn't a farm girl, far from it. An Irish Brooklyn girl, she was the epitome of a hoarder (much less than Eve was), as lots of folks turned out to be who'd suffered the Depression's scarcity. When I started working as Elaine's assistant—besides cleaning paint brushes and preparing manuscript pages for this other artist who wrote—one of my jobs was to help sort out Elaine's moun-tainous heaps of belongings that crammed her basement and attic, leaving only her spacious ground floor rooms to appear as if a *normal* person lived there.

Having ten or twelve of every pair of shoes, and duplicates of every dress, coat, trousers, scarf and blouse was not what an average person does. "I have to have them," Elaine simply told me. "Even though I know I'll never use them all. That's what being poor did to me."

My mom, just as poor when a child as Elaine, never hoarded clothes because she made all her own, even in her later years. Yet there were at least fifty pairs of old white tennis shoes in never-thrown-away bags in her house, found when things were being cleared out after her death, decades later. Eve's Depression scars were borne deeper within, marring her feelings of self-worth. Forcing her, I can only surmise, to *need to* put others down to feel better about herself rather than needing ten instead of just that one special lavender sweater, the way Elaine expressed her fear of lack.

I arrived in Elaine's life via an old fashioned, unsolicited letter, to which I'd attached a snapshot of myself kneeling in front of a recently completed art piece, a floor screen that depicted the ordinary-as-sacred, a male image on one side, a female on the other. Both sides of this life-size work jointly shared a clear quartz crystal, meant as a metaphor for a person's cerebral-spiritual headquarters, the mind. The double-pointed hand-length crystal was mounted in an oval cutout, right where both figures' heads, viewed from either side, would be. Maybe it's because in the photo I sent her, it was obvious I was a big strong woman, kneeling alongside this strong work of mine, and Elaine was small and, not exactly delicate, but not physically imposing as my height and work-muscles always have been. Or maybe it was my brazenly writing to ask the famous artist and art critic, de Kooning, if I could be her assistant—whichever it was, I got a phone call as soon as Elaine received my professionally formatted request for employment.

"I need someone to help me sort out my complicated life," a smoker's voice said through the receiver.

"I'm the one for you, Elaine," I confidently boasted. "Like you, I'm both artist and a writer. I know what it's like to have that kind of visual-literary duality going on, both sides of the brain stuff. I'm comfortable with all aspects of both approaches, trust me."

"When can you start?" she responded without hesitation.

I'd ended up in East Hampton straight from New York City, where I went after that year in Israel, after leaving Hawkeye and my addict's low life behind. In recovery now from my lifelong attempt to run away from everything, I arrived at Elaine's doorstep. Manhattan is where I'd had my so-called bottom, where I found relief from my desperate confusion; where I'd landed after thinking myself, for too long, both ex-pat and outcast.

I jumped into helping my amiable but overwhelmed new

employer sort through her ceiling-high, attic-filled, basement-crammed studio and house. I didn't know that Elaine, an acclaimed artist and art advocate, whose celebrity never interfered with our daily intimacy, was dying of cancer at the time. Yes, she had a bad cough, but she only scoffed whenever I expressed concern.

"I'm too busy to be sick," she said between gasps. "But yeah, they took out most of one lung last year. So what? I have paintings to paint, critiques and articles to write, and a contract for my memoirs to publish. There's simply no time for pity, so don't waste your breath. My life is full," the older woman who stood to my shoulders warned me with a wink. "So don't bother me with any nice concerns you might have, okay." Then Elaine had a coughing fit that interrupted her next sentence. As soon as the paroxysm abated, she picked up as if nothing had happened.

"I've got too many young artists, like you, teZa, to encourage," she said with a franticness that spoke far beyond her proven generosity.

If she was anything, Elaine was an encourager.

En-courage-er: someone who imparts courage to another, making others feel braver.

Eve, on the other hand, was too much of a worrier to have ever encouraged me to do anything creative—other than to get insurance.

Eve spoke directly now to Elaine as I stood watching in disbelief in my basement studio at the ludicrous scene before me: my two mothers, vying for my ... what? Loyalty? Certainly, not love because they must have known how much I loved each of them, despite both their strong opinions and desires to influence me about their particularly disparate worldviews.

"She's already defied her father and me," Mom was saying, "shunning our preference of her becoming a teacher. What more can we do, I ask you, Elaine, with this wild child of ours?

"And," Eve interjected for good measure, turning her eyes from her contemporary's to mine, yet speaking so loudly that Elaine couldn't mistake her insistent authority over me, "you *need* to get a more substantial job, *with insurance*, young lady! And a husband with those things, too!"

Eve never understood my love of art or any of the creations I made. Never expressed interest in reading any of my writing, either. I suppose because she was so engrossed in her own quite impressive creative output. Mother regarded both my sister and I solely as her *progeny*—our very being-ness she considered her own great achievements.

"Making art is something to be done only when the real work of life is complete," Eve had imposed upon me since childhood.

With Elaine—at whose doorstep I'd arrived a complete stranger—the two of us, mentor and apprentice, worked side-by-side for a year of what turned out to be the last in de Kooning's life. I catalogued her writings—that mountain of detritus that results from a famous artist's life, the clippings, notices of exhibitions, posters, international souvenirs and artifacts—I sorted and shipped it all off. Her so-called Inadvertent Collection of never-to-be-known artists went to the Women's Museum in our nation's capitol, along with the rest of her tchotchkes and artsy paraphernalia. Everything I sorted through she considered art-related, whether it was junk or treasure; a forty-year-old crisp, yellowed slip of paper announcing an Abstract Expressionist event, or the rare engraving by Picasso— Elaine treated everything equally as gold that was even in the slightest way related to the creative process.

As I worked she kept busy with her memoirs, preparing for her most current exhibition, and overseeing the care of her elderly estranged husband, Willem de Kooning, with whom she'd kept a close relationship throughout the decades of his loving other women. Just being with Elaine, at this early stage of re-entering real life (no more artificially induced stupors for me) solidified for me the same respectful, curiosity-fed awe of a life dedicated to creating, which her life was in every respect. I grew much stronger of heart, working with this multi-talented woman, learning to trust and love my role as both artist and writer, a person who desires to share about the ever-changing, upward-reaching possibilities of our collective human experience.

More from Elaine than H, more than from any of the rough 'n' tough sailors, buccaneers or boatswains, I learned about *courage* from this tiny woman clad in wispy black crepe, who wore ankle-length capes, who loved and nurtured me as her very own soul-daughter that beautiful year we spent working together. She gave me the healing I needed from not having had a supportive birth-mother, Eve, who turned out to be my toughest adversary, judge, jury and executioner, for my wanting to make art, she who bore me into this world. On my side now, I had a second, soul-mom: Elaine, who rooted for me instead of condemned me for having turned out so different from the way my birth-mother wanted.

I looked at the two women as they stood sparring in my East Hampton low-ceilinged, neon-lit studio. Facing off, having cross words—over me.

"I'm telling you she needs a real profession, with benefits," my tall stiff mother insisted.

"And I'm repeating, Eve," short graceful Elaine softly stated, "that to someone like teZa, thinking that way will kill her curious wild-child spirit."

"What do you mean?" Eve sounded angry. "How can it kill someone to have insurance?"

"Because," Elaine said, "if that's the main objective of a person's life, to have insurance, or rely on anything other than one's own creative, driving force, your daughter will never be able to make moving, strong, totally original art. Which hers is, in spades. She'll just be an ordinary person, not who she really is. Having insurance will give her false security. She, and all of us creative sorts, we need to feel on the razor's edge all the time. We artists have different needs than ordinary people. We're … different."

I looked at my two mothers. How I loved them both! Elaine,

with her soft billowing noir clothes that moved like raven wings as she swung her expressive limbs akimbo. And visiting-from-the-burbs, pastel-clad Eve, with her polyester pants suit, feet and hands firmly placed as if in formation for battle. Both women stood implacable. Both of them victims, themselves, of the Great Depression's hardships. Elaine hoarded clothes. Eve hoarded her opinions.

Clearly, the one who'd never had a child of her own was the one now able to give me the mothering, nurturing comfort I'd yearned for all my life. My existence as a rogue artist had always been lonely, I admit. Elaine was giving me the peer acceptance I'd always sought, and had thought unattainable, before arriving on her doorstep. I loved Elaine, especially for this, besides giving me a generous weekly paycheck, sans insurance.

Eve—yes, she'd given me life, the most important gift of all. For that alone, I stood in awe before her, bowing to the biological wonder of birth she'd bestowed upon me, with my dad's help of course. Added to that, my gratitude for Eve's giving me such a good, wholesome foundation, the multiple ways she made me feel well-grounded and prepared, the result of her practical influences of a farm girl's daughter that she showered on me every moment of my carefree youth—before everything changed.

Yet as a grown woman, Eve's love for me had so many mandates, strings, conditions, and expectations, I knew I could never live up to them. Because her idea of who I am, and what the purpose of my life is, wasn't real. Her expectations were Eve's, not mine. But Elaine's recognition of me, as her artistic, creative equal, felt like nonstop gush to me. She treated me with a just-right formula of no-nonsense *simpatico*, recognizing in me a free spirit just like her own, freeing me more than any other female's nurturing had ever done.

On that remarkable day when both Elaine and Eve hovered over me—the two most important female role models in my life, debating what was best for the fledgling ugly duckling I thought I was—one interested in me and the original work I *was making*; the other concerned about me only because she'd *made me*—it was an intense showdown.

I stayed in a far corner, in a shadow of my studio space, observing. This was an hour-long battle of control vs. letting-go, between *what-is* and *what-ain't*. I saw the raw discrepancy between my two mothers, so abundantly obvious just by listening to their words. I didn't need an intuitive kick in the gut to figure out who was really on my side, who celebrated my hard-earned freedom as artist and independent person, and who wanted to proclaim total ownership over my very existence.

Seeing how two such similar cuts of female, born at the same time in history, and how they impacted my world and others around them, in such very different ways, made me at that moment not utter a word, because I was so enthralled.

With my eyes and ears, I could finally see and hear the truth. That my own mother didn't know who I was. That she never had, not since I started growing from her baby to the person I was meant to be. In contrast, Elaine, whom I'd met just that past year, knew me in and out, in a deeply profound way, one in which Eve never even considered about either of her children.

While Elaine was dead from cancer within the next year, Eve would live another thirty. Not knowing Elaine was so ill, I had moved away to Florida. After hearing of my mentor's death, I was told by a mutual acquaintance that Elaine, hallucinating as her end drew near, was found dazed, wandering the hall outside her Southampton, New York hospice room, asking everyone she met, "Where's teZa?"

I was touched when I was told this, soon after Elaine's passing.

Touched by how closely she'd held me, her last studio assistant, in her heart. Surely, like a daughter, I like to think. Both of us needed each other, at exactly that moment in our lives. She needed to mother me as much as I needed her to.

Happily, Elaine bestowed life-changing confidence upon me, her spiritual daughter; the kind of care my own mother couldn't give because, sadly, she had none leftover to give away. It would take me, much later, to be with Eve at the end of her life, to realize this truth of how she did her best.

At middle age, in youth, or at the very end of life—it's never too late to have a change of heart. Any one of us, with awareness of *what is*, can change a lack into an opportunity to find whatever it is we need to feel more complete. With Elaine's encouraging, starting from our very first connection, I changed from feeling cursed, a victim of being misunderstood, crippled by *rejectionitis*, to the Self-accepting person I'd once been.

I don't hold one mother higher than the other. They both gave me different aspects of a mother's true love. Elaine—who spiritually helped heal my damaged soul—impacted my life as much as being brought into this world, Eve's job. During our short time together, Elaine acted as if she'd been waiting for me to come, to help her prepare to die, to help her organize her stored-up, hoarded life's accumulation. When Elaine received my stamped-envelope letter in the mail—with the wild crazy photo I'd inserted of me next to my person-sized foldout screen, with the shared diamond-crystal bright center, with my eighties-style punk hair spiked out in electrocuted platinum streaks—that day forever changed both our lives.

And Eve? After that freaky duel over my well-being in my basement studio that day, when we were finally alone later, she quickly dismissed Elaine as "a famous goofball," before retreating to her isolated fisherwoman's existence back at her home in Florida.

Eve, however, who would live to ninety-seven, grew to be an equally prized treasure of mine, as Elaine had been earlier. In time, I would come to appreciate the solid base of knowledge she'd given me, in such great measure, fit for a life dedicated to seeking Spirit as mine became. Good, basic earthy stuff, Eve gave me. Just like all those eggs Grammom Antonina, her mom, fed the Depression wanderers. Eve, an immigrant's daughter, fed her own two offspring good wholesome strength, and a healthy dose of tenacity needed by anyone to enjoy a well-rounded, happy life.

Both mothers' magic wands of caring helped me become brave enough to spread more love. Both helped me learn to love my better, higher Self, first. Eve taught me how to feed and clothe my physical body, and inspired my intellect's education. Elaine showed me how to feed my Spirit, how to let my creative Self fly free from restraints of conformity. Even from needing to have insurance.

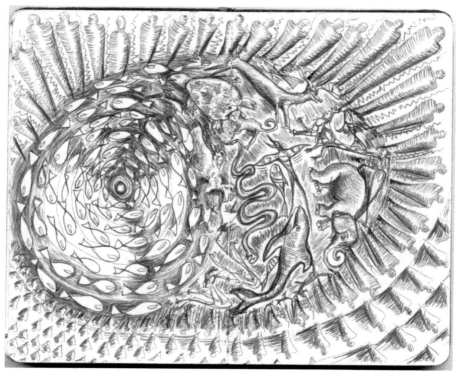

look more closely to better understand adaptation

CHAPTER 10

the messiness of loving

Silver glints, swift pulsations of easeful movements: fish in the sea
Gliding, following current and weather systems, seasons, avoiding
predators
Consumed to near-depletion
No fishing in Newfoundland, land of fishermen
Japanese and Russian motherships
Fish factories raping the seas illegally
Moratoriums, regulations, protections
And still, fish survive despite ravages of humans
Breathing gills, adapting, sometimes perishing
Will a human ever know the mind of a fish?
Will a fish ever know the mind of a human?
Regarded as home, this planet should have been named Water, not
Earth
And for that alone, fish, and other inhabitants of the waters of Earth
Are the true inheritors of the planet
Will they survive after we humans are gone?
Will they share with us their secret of longevity?
Fossils and future species, evolving to adapt
Survivors are the hybrid vigors of extinct fish families
Yes, humans, look more closely at the cold-blooded fish
To better understand adaptation
At its best

In the background a sacred chant is playing softly. Her breath still moves through her, unlike times before when it's stopped for long pauses in the days and weeks leading up to this moment, here.

Today is the day of the fisherwoman, my pagan mama's leaving this earthly world.

Eve is tired of being human. She's sick of this worn out, nearly hundred-year-old body of hers. She's readying to take off and fly away. As a good Christian-pagan (which all Lithuanian Catholics are in their hearts) she'd already made known years ago, her wish of how she wants to come back, as an oak tree. Already, Eve is greeting the other Unseens who have been arriving, gathering here to escort her. A few try to scare her, admittedly, but … I chase them away, to stop them from bothering Eve, using my weapon of choice, the Light of my love.

All her life Eva Maria, named for the first good girl and the first bad girl, as she always liked to tell people, she'd been a feisty adventurer. In the wake of her huge appetite for life, she did things unheard of for her time, especially for a woman of such poverty-impinged roots. From subsistence farmer parents, she escaped and married Linwood.

My father was a *tall drink of water*, a sax player, "That gangster from Camden," Grammom would say. He, with a Camel-and-whiskey smooth singing voice, was a jazz sax musician, an amateur heavyweight boxer, a big bad scary repo-man who'd put his younger sister through college, without thinking twice that he himself couldn't afford to go. He had to work. When his two girls came along, my sister and I, Dad transformed from a jaunty too-tall submariner into a traveling salesman who always paid his bills on time. A good man, putting his family first.

I had attended Linwood's deathbed, too. A much simpler, calmer affair than this farewell Eve is resisting. My role, like it'd also been for Dad's passing, was to be the bridge tender, the keeper of the flame, the recorder of the Light as it came hovering closer to

Mom's struggling form, these last few days, hours, minutes, of her life here.

What makes the passage of one's essence back to where we come from, for some of us, so Light-filled, so sublime, while for others there are fights with unseen demons right up to the moment of one's last breath? Linwood's journey back to the *Source of All* was via cancer, and, like most diseases, there was a beginning, middle, and an end to his farewell, a drama that got strewn about in the messy wake of death's physical warfare. Cancer is, if it's anything, war within an individual's body, between dark and light, good and bad, white and red corpuscles, too-few healthy versus too-many-deadly cancer cells.

Eve's journey back to the Light was not from a disease, like Dad's. Her body was worn out. Her heart was unsure about what lay ahead. Her Source, the Source of All, the *Light of consciousness* (as I call *It*), became covered by murky layers that she had to sort out, bit by bit, by slowly releasing all parts of herself, freeing things inside that she'd never been able to let go of controlling. She had to do this before Eve allowed herself—that part of her beyond her body and mind—to release, allowing *It* to be at peace.

In order to do this, she needed me at her side. Mother resisted though, and fought my help up to the end. But after she lost all conscious control, yet still resisted, she needed my help to get to the other side. Through the portal of the living to the other side of consciousness, to where all shadows get un-darkened, when the pure Light of recognition is shown to be … the Unseens.

Soon enough, Eve reached the shore of her final peace. But not before, once again, as she did throughout her long life, she went through all the negatives she allowed more space in her heart than necessary. The many un-wanteds, un-forgivables that Eve found atrocious about others. Not herself. Just *others*.

To my way of thinking, this over-concern with others' behavior had always been such a waste of precious time. Eve could have been a lot more comfortable in life had she chosen not to judge, if she could have realized she didn't need to control so much. Everyone has that choice: have a hard time anywhere, anytime; or choose to have a joyous lounge on the beach of life's eternal sunshine.

Life is what we make of it. The Unseens who gather as death draws near, remind us of that.

Having helped both my parents through the invisible portal separating the living from the dead, the only thing I know for certain is that the energy of existence beckons us to make our own life, uniquely ours. Some make it as comfortable as we can; others insist on seeing life as nothing more than beastly bad business; at the most, something to be endured. For me the truth, since attaining release from self-destructive addictions—is that life *It-self* is a gift. The choice of how we view our life is for each person to make for themselves.

Eve chose to never investigate what it was like to stand tall and proud, and explore the Light of consciousness, as she had explored the Taj Mahal, Macchu Pichu, or other worldly exotic places. She simply didn't believe in *It*.

How, I asked myself, *could she have forgotten how she comforted me when I needed it, when I had that dream about being dead, as a young child?*

The Light, Love, whatever one calls the Source—Spirit—"It can't be that damn simple, Linduta," she'd say to me, annoyed I'd asked *again* if she had faith in the Unseen, unknowable Mystery, as she drew nearer to *It*. Eve just didn't want to discuss "that stuff." Not ever. Especially not during those final eighteen months, when I was her near-constant helpmate. Her Catholic religion was all she wanted to know, all she believed to be True. Heaven awaited her. God the Father, Son, and Holy Ghost, and Mary, the Holy Mother, her namesake and her main Divine Interceptor, were all that Mom needed. Religion was all she could believe in, beginning from her simple upbringing, on to when she became a busy young wife and mother; and during each of her many incandescent roles in her life's great drama. Mom's life was dedicated to sharing what she knew with others, not exploring an unknown, unseen realm never exposed to her in her religion or autodidact studies.

Eve figured as long as she was in control of how she and others felt, everything was bound to be good. And oh, did she enjoy life! She had no need to know the Light, she claimed. The "light," whether of universal consciousness or a simple bulb in an electric fixture, didn't impact her life enough for her to want to know the source of its origin. *Enjoyable*, for her, and *Life Eternal*, meant the same thing to her: following The Commandments of the Most Holy Church of Rome. These rules were solid, and safe for her, guaranteed by the Pope, attained by receiving the Holy Sacraments, and blessed by wafts of heavenly incense, these guidelines that promised their adherents nothing short of eternal salvation.

But on that final day, at the side of my dear mama's deathbed, Eve was no longer in control.

What is it that makes it so hard for us humans to turn away from love, even when it's caused irreparable, lifelong damage, such as well-meaning, but controlling parents do to their innocent, guileless children? From the moment I announced I wanted to explore creativity as a teenager, Eve disapproved of me choosing the path that life compelled me to take.

When I decided to be an artist, having herself never been given that option while growing up as a poor farm girl, instead of wishing her daughter well and telling me "You can do it!" Eve shouted, "There's no money in *that*!"

Even after a lifetime of being criticized, told I couldn't be who I knew I had to be, I still did as all good daughters do, I stayed by Eve's bedside, forgiving her, trying to understand my mother had to do what she did because … that was *her story*.

Eve never thought anything I did was worthwhile, not until I got married, when, at the age of forty-four, I took up the role of being *Angel Mom* to my husband's two young kids. *That*, Eve could relate to. "Finally, you're doing something with your life," she'd told me, but only after the first ten years of our marriage had passed. The years before then, well, Eve was certain I was going to be just as much a failure as a mom as she thought I'd been with everything else.

What she didn't realize, however, was that my actual successes were anchored in the very things that Mom had taught me as a youngster. To love Nature. To laugh and toss my head at the impossible, turn away from naysayers and forget the negatives: focus on the positives. To grow and make things, constantly, without effort, without money being the reason why. To joke and thumb my nose, and strut right up to the face of life's harsh realities—like Eve always did.

"Always try your very best," I remember Mom telling us. It was Eve who taught me to pack just a toothbrush and take off on an adventure, without a care or a change of clothes, not to bother with much else other than to tame my wild hair into a neat braid before setting out to explore this big wide world, to seek its truths, speak with as many of its inhabitants as I could, and to drink of its endlessly enriching ways.

"And never stop till your feet wear off your legs," Mom added. Which mine haven't yet, as hers have.

People might think this is a weird love story, reporting as I am, sitting at my mother's deathbed, while Eve, already unconscious, breathes her last shallow lung-fulls. Eve is almost at peace. Her need to overachieve has faded, already died. Her well-worn saddle has been finally, against her wishes, hung up on its hook; her wild ride through life—has come to an end. The grand finale of Eve's boisterous journey here on Earth, is happening right now. Instead of her old self anticipating her next, her best earthly adventure, there are no more left. The hospice nurses are now administering morphine to stifle Mom's pain. She doesn't have cancer. She's just old. So what kind of pain could be causing Eve such distress as we're witnessing?

In Eve's case, she never had the desire or the courage to combat the demons that prevented her from recognizing the Light within her own Self. In her stubborn clinging to the belief that her Catholic religion was the only insurance policy she needed for the afterlife, her veritable free ticket into heaven, she felt she had all she needed to safeguard herself from any evil influence. Yet these personal devils of hers hovered insistently around her, even as she was preparing to leave her physical body. Crowding her, making it hard for her to concentrate on the joy of leaving this difficult world.

Before, when she was semi-conscious, she tried to bat them away with her arms flailing, outstretched, trying to keep the invisible troublemakers away from her. They persisted, but the demons failed to push aside the angel, Eve's personal Unseen, who called herself Wanda, who came to sit by Eve Mary's side the other night. The night nurse, a woman of vision, or *Sight* as some like to say, saw Wanda sitting there as Eve struggled with the pestering gnat-like demonic tormentors that hovered around her deathbed.

Unlike Mom, I was forced to combat my personal demons, of which I'd had plenty. I had to do this demon-killing as part of "the work" I was guided to do, back when I chose to live a sober life, a life a teacher of mine described as "living in the Light." I was shown I had to live as close to the Light of Truth as I possibly could, so its brilliance would scare away those demons I'd had.

Some people call these demons the *shadow side* of a person. Jungian psycho babble, but that term will do.

In the bedroom in which Mom had nested for the previous thirty years, everything is silent except for the low volume sacred chant I've been playing for three days straight. I am respectfully, silently observing the miracle of Life's greatest event, Death, that's unfolding before us, right now. Mom, she can't speak anymore. Everything about her is gone but for her breath, which comes less and less often now. I know she senses something. I got up close and stared right into her open clear, emerald green eyes I've always loved looking into, as she lay in her last experiences of that sense, of sight. She's made no contact with anyone outside her inner Self for hours, but suddenly Mom *pushed me away* from her ... the final use of her crumbling temple's last great effort; physically signaling to me I was the pest she'd often told me I was.

Her silence might have been forced upon her, but her last words to me had been evidence of her not realizing how close she was to leaving us. She hadn't meant to say something mean. But ... she'd never bothered to eradicate that nasty speech-demon that lived inside her. She quietly sobbed when she realized how cruel her final words had been to me, right after saying them. I soothed her.

"Mom, you can't help it. Try to relax," I said. "I'm not going to leave you. Don't worry."

Then, there were no more remarks of heart-crushing criticism, no more disapprovals after the next step took away her reason, her senses, as well as her voice, clamping her mouth shut.

At the moment I'm painting for you, doubtless the pestering demons bothering Mom were being criticized by her, perhaps being bargained with, her hustling them for more time, for more space, more something. Her speech gone, Eve could only communicate with the Spirits that hovered around her bed. Disjointed, disembodied, Eve alone saw them. Wanda, was she there? I do not have *the Sight* so I couldn't say.

Later, the assisting hospice nurse asked me, "Did you see that glass that whooshed across your mom's tray by itself? I've never felt so many weird presences in a person's room, as with your mom."

I tried to comfort Mom as she lay, her labored breathing coming, ever so slowly, to an end. I whispered in her ear, "Mom, you and I are going through this, together."

It was true. I was there, gladly, to help her to the other side. I figured if I wasn't there, Eve would suffer much more, and I couldn't allow that. I felt my role was as companion, a comforting one to her, guiding her silently, praying for her, singing sweetly, softly, along with the soothing familiar yogic chant I played for her, knowing how much it comforts.

Behind the veil of illusion that only the dead or dying can see through, is where she's headed, I thought. *This is her last great adventure and I'm pleased to assist her, if I can. She's allowed me to do so little for her, and she'd done so much for me. Now, I have this chance, here. She's having a hard time, poor baby mommy. All those decades of her telling me I can't do this or that, haven't worked. I didn't believe her. And lucky for her, now, because I've learned how to Love, enough for her, enough for anyone who needs more.*

I am loving my doubting-mom to the other side. Through the abyss of dark phantoms that she had mumbled so uneasily about these last days. I'd hear a word, a fragment, like 'sled,' 'cabbage,' 'box'—her angry fists surprisingly able to hit the air when all else of her body seemed liquefied before my eyes, sinking into the mattress. In between her combat, she sighed, grimaced, whistled, moaned—everything but showing signs of the awe Dad's passing was washed with. I knew she had to be deluged by some sort of demons.

I will be my mother's remedy. I am the joy that has somehow gone amiss from her earthly life. She created me. I am part of her and she is part of me. Joy is what she intended, but could not hold onto. Joy is the state in which she and my father conceived me. "You're a love child," they'd both claimed. Although Mom herself could never truly believe in joy, no matter how hard I or anyone tried to share it with her. Instead, she would challenge, argue, put down, and diss any form of the Light ever shared or offered her,

outside of her free-pass-to-heaven Christianity insurance policy.
That's why she never liked my art. Too much of a throwback to
paganism for her, seeing Spirit everywhere, in everything, as I do.

And now, at the final hour of her life—my love for her, pure and
real and this death before us, the reverse of her having borne me—
I am happy to help her into the Light.

As her breath becomes shallower, I hold Mom's limp hand as I
bring her closer, closer to the Light. And then ... I lead her right into
It, handing her over to the blinding Source. Her body shudders with
the last death rattle, a frightening sound, a worthy ending of a full
and perfect life, for her. Joy awaited her, at last. I know this because
I witnessed her safe arrival.

Wanda, Eve's angel, hovered around my mother and me,
protecting us, giving us strength to go through this most difficult of
life's challenges: witnessing up close the final life-passage of a
loved one. I stayed at Mother's side, now completely still. I can no
longer help her. I can only watch as Wanda guides Mom's spirit
further, right into the blinding Light *It-self.* Now it's Mom's time to
experience Oneness. I think back to the time, when I was very
young, when she helped me to remember this feeling, after
mistaking it for death as I had, in my childhood's horrible
nightmare.

I remain still and observe Mom's stillness. How beautiful she
looks, finally at peace.

I know helping Mom was part of my role; as is helping others
wherever fear paralyzes or hinders, uncovering whenever the Light
gets hidden by arrogance, masked by fear, mistaken for something
else, confused or denied.

Life, like Love, often isn't very pretty. Sometimes it gets
distorted from what we imagined it'd be like. Wildly disparate
flavors and kaleidoscopic facets of this brilliance called Life keep
us who are aware of *It,* whether hybrid vigors or old-fashioned homo

sapiens, all trying to know Love a little better, in all its myriad forms. And in the process, we'll have a more fulfilling time of living, knowing we are always a part of the Source. In the trying *to know Love* we bring joy a little nearer to our own hearts right now, this present moment at hand.

CHAPTER 11

amazed and astounded

Toward the Light! The war cry of moths, not just awakened humans!

We must, we must, we must seek the Light! All moths know this, feel this, and never question this urge. Just as they know they must eat holes in wool garments, or munch the host-plant their eggs get laid upon, flying moths know they must follow the Light; but for what purpose, no one really knows. A moth, like a butterfly, spends its earlier life in other forms. Both butterflies and moths are true examples of metamorphosis, shape-shifting; the biological, chronological changing that happens to all living creatures, in various measures, within their life span.

The moth emerges from its cocoon (as a caterpillar emerges from its chrysalis) in its adult, mate-able form, totally different from the tiny eggs the mature female will lay after mating. Each tiny egg hatches into its larva stage, then matures into its wormlike pupa form in which it soon is surrounded by its self-made protective cocoon; from which, in time, all adult moths emerge—to again mate, eat, poop, lay eggs and—to search out light.

Seeking the light, any light, is as much a part of a moth's existence as feeding, mating, and laying more eggs during its short time of existence.

Besides the innate need to seek physical light—be it the self-annihilating flame of a candle or the orb of an outdoor electric lightbulb—does a moth have the Light of consciousness within it, as we humans do?

Well, of course! All creatures have *It*! This is how the expression, "the Light in their eyes" became the litmus test for proclaiming life, versus the unlit eyes of death. Creatures of all sorts, have Light within them. Some manifest through the light reflected in their eyes. Others, like the lower creatures, a moth for instance, seeks the Light through outer means because ... Light is familiar, it's desirable ... they want *It*.

A species' need to navigate may have something to do with this compulsion to seek out illumination, but that theory has not yet been proven as the reason why moths hunger for light in the dark of night. Lepidopterists who study both moths and butterflies, think there's a natural photoactive, light-sensitive mechanism within members of the moth family, causing them to naturally seek out luminosity in darkness. Whether moths use light as a form of geographic orientation, or what other reason this light-attraction is for, no one knows for certain.

A moth's obsession might possibly be analogous to why certain humans seek the Light of Knowledge? Because to a moth ... Light *feels good!* ... just as to a seeker of Truth, the knowledge that all life is interconnected is so comforting, soothing, and rewarding. Every creature, of every description, every living entity, whether dirt-chomping earthworm or a truly enlightened person—does things to make them feel good, to keep them alive, and serves their particular purpose for *being*.

A moth may sometimes have to sacrifice its life when it dives into the light of a campfire. But wait, don't lament! Perhaps it's ready to evolve into the next level of Being, and wants to die. Has to die, in fact, in order to be released from its lower form. These kinds of unanswerable questions are part of the Great Mystery of Life. These are things the Unseens, our trusted guides urge us humans to ask of ourselves or our trusted others. When we ask such questions, we must listen carefully to answers, when they arrive.

Some of us humans act moth-like, seeking out the Light even knowing we might be called on to sacrifice our life in order to imbibe, and share, the bliss of its knowledge.

On that long-ago day, when I unloaded my old art pieces at the festive tent erected for recyclables at the East Hampton dump, I felt I was diving into a consuming, life-altering light of some kind, giving away my life's work like I was. It felt like I was experiencing some kind of dying, but at the same time I was simultaneously being reborn. This radical act of mine, disposing of my life's work (up to that point), was a ritual I devised to honor my commitment to, from then on, live according to a higher code of ethics. Finally, I was ready to let go of what didn't work for me any longer, and create a new reality for myself. I was practicing "being in the Light" by ridding myself of my old dark art works, throwing them out along with the old destructive habits of drinking, drugging and acting stupid, focused only on my own wants. I decided to "seal," to "make holy" this new reality of mine by sending all my "babies" to oblivion—releasing my creative offspring, which took years of effort to make. From that day on, I would never make anything depicting ugly, self-negating feelings, but only hypnotically beautiful and shockingly weird, I hoped. I would create strong, edgy images strangely juxtaposed: making the viewer wonder: Huh? That day at the dump, I was truly rebirthing myself.

Through this simple act of recycling my negative-themed creations at the dump, I declared my old self dead and my new life, Self-born in its place. By my own intention, I *became* a new, better, highly improved hybrid vigor specimen of my former self.

I know, this all sounds very fantastical. However, this is the way I see life: as magical, replete with ever-changing possibilities, a Mystery unsurpassable and unknowable—and more than anything, entertaining—like good fun is. The instant I chose to rebirth myself into a being of Light I felt released from the stifling, doomed-for-annihilation smallness of the previous use of my life-energy allotment. No longer was I looking for *It*. I willed my Self to become One with *It*.

Guided by my whispers now more than ever, listening to my now-trusted inner Voice, even communicating with *It* via Noname, my personal Unseen, whenever I had a question, or wanted another, higher perspective—I now knew all things were possible. Technicalities aside, I did re-birth myself that day at the dump. I consciously rid my life of all that was holding me back, that came before I had learned how to love my own inner Self.

I managed to do this just by wanting to. I re-birthed a new improved version of my old self. A hybrid vigor—my true, inner Self—was at last freed!

It was 1984 when I was finally ready to get real, get honest, and put behind me the previous decades of Self-annihilation. Two years before visiting the dump, I'd decided to get sober. But when I took my old bad-art babies to the dump and watched perfect strangers claim them, dragging them away—and felt the surreptitious joy of seeing others claim that old art of mine as fast as they could, scurrying away with their loot—that's when I began to live, truly live, my life's purpose. My old former self, the weak victim who could only be scared of who I really was—was now dead.

There was nothing left but the photos I had taken of my previous artwork, those pre-sober, feeble attempts ... of *Fear* trying to beat up *Trust*.

I never regretted throwing all that crap away, not for a second.

The same that happened to me at the Southampton dump can happen to every single person. Challenges abound, within our own selves and outside us. Whether in people's or a government's actions, fear creates chaos and turmoil. Having endured it, then cast it aside, myself, I can attest that pain, especially the emotional type

I was plagued by, is as real as a ripe fruit that falls from its tree.

Evil, once it's been identified, must be eradicated. Eliminating the type of demons that live in the mind-body-and-soul, takes effort. Once recognized, un-useful energy, or inner demons can be wiped out. How? By exposing them to the Light of higher, purer consciousness.

For me, I took on the mixed signals of my childhood situation, the mixed messages I got from our culture, and let the "lacks" I'd been subjected to dictate too much my grown-up character. Because I had no role model before that time to show me any other options.

When nurturers, whether inadvertently or intentionally, negatively affect a child's development, it's up to the grownup that child inevitably becomes, to make right the shortcomings of their caretakers. This takes Self-effort, also known as Self-Awareness.

When children are victimized, like in the spate of school shootings that has happened in my beleaguered country—surely this is a sign that human culture has become plagued by demons. Random violence is evil personified. Fear within an individual pulls the trigger and ends up killing innocents. The antidote to Fear is Love. It's up to us to help heal all evils with spreading more Love; to make compassionate Love the next, most popular fad that everyone talks about, about which movies and shows and songs are made, and celebrities rave over—and then, with the force of Love, we successfully turnaround the deep state of distrust into which our family of humankind has sunk so low.

When people believe and focus more on fear than Love's creative solutions, we cannot heal our world. We heal a culture by healing our Self first. How can we trust the Light of consciousness to save us at this crossroads of evolution that we're at right now?

I can only speak from my own experiences. Everything started to change when I became courageous enough to admit that I was delusional, and could see that fear only existed within myself. That's when I was forced to make the choice: take action to dissolve the fear that had ruled my life, or die. I had no plan, and certainly didn't know much about the higher type of Love, which begins with Self Love, before I committed to re-birthing myself as a hybrid vigor.

An extreme event, a tragedy so profound had to occur in my own life, that the only choice I had was to die, or change myself— seriously, that was my only choice. Having the *last* in my serial-breakdowns, with friends finally audial-taping me in a state of vile, evil possession, then insisting on playing that tape over and over until my thick wall of denial came crumbling down, was an experience utterly humiliating, and so ... mortifying. But it forced me to Wake Up! No matter what it's called, a mental, physical, or spiritual breakdown, a psychic shock, an addict's bottom, a do-or-die crisis, social unrest, or a tragic terminal disease—life inevitably presents a crossroads to all who need to change. One in which we're presented a choice: either spiritualize our life, or lose our precious grasp of life's joy.

We demand change! Now's the time we have to be willing to work for what we want. We ask, "Do we want to live?" and if the answer is "Yes!" we must change. Quickly we must prepare to battle the demons of despair. We strengthen ourselves to make known to everyone that evil does not deserve to reside on earth without a damn good fight. We who have either chosen or been forced to conquer our own demons, must help others not to hide from theirs any longer. The time of blaming others is over. We ourselves have the power to change, within ourselves.

My hybrid vigor Self can at last say this.

I started thinking this way as soon as I returned back to my studio from the dump after letting-go of my demon-tortured works. The packrats who'd made off with their loot, my precious life's work, now owned all that angst-filled art, not me. My new Self gave me its first pep talk:

Express the fear, speak about it, don't hide it anymore. In this way, by exposing it to the Light, fear is dissipated, simply because it's no longer allowed to be hidden within a hopeless heart.

Do not pretend fear doesn't exist. If we see, hear, or feel someone to be mentally in a fragile, dangerous state of murderous rage, it's our responsibility to get involved, to take appropriate action to ward off evil's looming rampage. Ask that person if they want help. Then go get help for any disturbed person. Hybrid vigors speak our fears aloud, because they are no longer hidden, but honestly shared with others. When fears are outed, they can't run and hide and disappear from the Light with so many people pointing at them, no longer afraid of Fear itself.

We can no longer afford to pretend fear doesn't exist. Our job as hybrid vigor humans is to celebrate great and glorious things, yes! But also, to face the shadow of evil that lurks beneath the outermost layer of everyday life. Identify fear first, then call it what it is—demonic. Then prepare to do battle to slay the demons, the darkness of our world. One by one, each of us will conquer the demons within, until they are all gone.

Bringing Fear out of its deeply hidden places, into the Light, is the cure for evil of all kinds.

Awakened to the hybrid vigor Self, each of us can help the other to heal, to re-build trust, to mend our brokenness. As hybrid vigors, we can admit that fear must be spoken about, neither sensationalized, nor internalized. Only then we'll come to trust that Love is much stronger than hate, one of Fear's other names.

Like the physical light that moths are drawn to, the Light of Love, our Oneness consciousness draws each of us to be stronger. Our perceptions are guided to become more awake and aware than any of us ever thought we were capable of being.

We must never pretend that all is well when our society has become so fraught with fear, so weak with demoralizing debasement. Every bit of energy we spend to help heal our human condition is worth the endeavor Self-effort takes, a million times over.

Humankind's fate is in the hands of we awakened hybrid vigors.

Here's how:

First, we firmly believe our world—its environment and humankind's social structures—are completely heal-able.

Life's darkness has been revealed. Whether via another mass shooting, or bizarre political event that resembles the funny papers more than the regal diplomacy of international affairs, the time for change has come. Just as destructive storms hurt geographical places in which their violent forces hit, everything in Nature mends and evolves, in time. Likewise, it's true that every flawed individual can be healed, in time. And it stands just as logically, then, that an entire culture also can become more balanced. One person at a time.

Hybrid vigors make this choice to heal, first ourselves, then our collective world. We are ready to take the giant leap to our next step in humanity's spiritual evolution.

Send healing wherever it's needed. Even to the most deranged, hopeless individual. Even to a scary leader whose volatile unattractive nature nobody trusts, whose megalomania scares the living daylights out of any sane person.

The group is much greater than any one individual. We, the Seens, and the Unseens—we are all connected. Our collective power to heal is—unlimited. Openness, honesty, and transparency will heal the tear in the fabric of our infected world, which peoples' hidden fears have caused. Oneness is a gigantic weaving of not just humanity, but all in existence, including animals and other sentient and inanimate beings, plants, minerals, the elements of earth, water, fire, and sky. Our planet and beyond is as alive as any of us are.

With our combined psychic energies focused, anything's possible. We can spread the balm of Love as surely as some try to deny its existence or its relevance, as some cynics persist in claiming.

There is a bridge from our world of Seen things, to that of the

Unseen dimensions. A bridge we can freely cross over at will, any time. By slowing our thoughts, stilling our minds, and following our breath, we cross this bridge. This is how we tune into the Light of consciousness: through focusing on our breath, which is our internal bridge between our lower and higher selves.

After experiencing both sides, both choices, a higher perspective and a lower, anyone will agree that Fear leads nowhere but to self, or society's uncomfortable disintegration and ultimately, to the destruction of joy.

Choose to not just live your life, but to live the highest experience you possibly can.

Together, we can heal any darkness by focusing on the Light. Speaking uplifting, kind words to one another is how we can start. Spread joy and hope. Say no to fear, blame, and prolonged anger. It takes practice, I won't kid you. Changing fear into trust is the only way we will cure the epidemic of separation that has infected us worldwide.

Speak "Help" aloud or silently, and listen to what you receive back. Then, take immediate action. Guidance is always here, right within us. Just ask.

Allow yourself to become a hybrid vigor, here and now. This is the future of humankind's survival.

Infinitely expanding love is more delicious than anything any of us could have imagined possible.

Like a moth diving into the deadly allure of a fire's flame, the Light of Love too, is worth dying for, in the process of experiencing *It* fully. Experience *It* instead of denying *It*, running from *It*, or trying to control *It*.

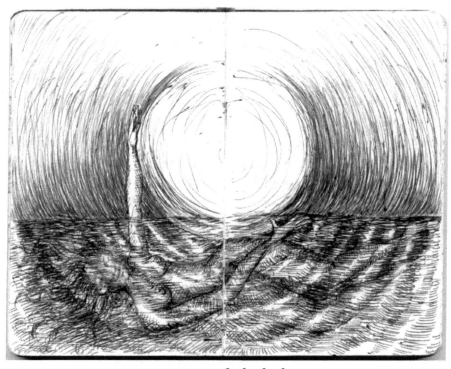

we must seek the light

CHAPTER 12

being a hybrid vigor

Our human family is becoming blended, far beyond the racism and xenophobia of the past. When people inter-breed—blacks with whites, Jews with Arabs, and every other conceivable mixture—that new inter-bred human loses their sense of belonging to a specific race, or feeling disenfranchised, losing both inferiority and superiority in the process. Only now, as we mix biologically and culturally more and more, the combined resources of our actual blendedness refocuses from competing amongst ourselves to a much more expanded, more creatively productive era.

In this time now, when terrible and wonderful are both so prevalent, we as a species, are learning to relax. Those of us who define ourselves as *spiritual human beings* are most likely to experience true mental-physical-emotional freedom. When the vast majority of the world's population becomes a homogenous skin shade—one in which individuals are no longer pure white, black, yellow or red, and that day is coming sooner than most people think—that's when we can truly call ourselves a worldwide *blended* family of humankind. It's happening already. That's why citizens from compass points all over the globe can now begin to think about real issues, and *do* the important work—like healing the Earth's toxic environment. This shift is already happening in great numbers.

Making the choice to elevate ourselves, to be open to a more enlightened perspective, a radical change of consciousness, makes the difference between feeling doomed or having faith that new possibilities are available to all of us, with no exceptions. Every single one of us can decide to change and become more than we ever thought possible.

We *can repair* the planet's skin and its atmosphere, just as our own body can heal. To heal, one needs time, rest, and wholesome nurturing. The planet, indeed the entire universe, is the macrocosm of our own body's microcosm. Individuals must heal themselves before the planet ever will. Healing tools are being revealed to us, to some more quickly than others—but they are within each person's reach. Every so-called *mistake* a person, or a culture has ever been through, becomes an opportunity for growth. In the same way that many of us *do recover* individually from dis-eases and addictions and other chronic or deadly conditions, we now are collectively healing our planet's sick environment as well as our toxic human culture, simply because enough individuals have healed themselves, and have now become more whole and balanced. Way more hybrid vigors exist now than earlier in my lifetime. Each year, the tsunami of Love seems to grow higher, wider, more crowded with enthusiastic seekers.

Countless people have already re-birthed themselves as hybrid vigors, or are in the process. People old and young are now, or soon about to, coming up with solutions to modern life's many life-threatening challenges. New sustainable sources of energy are being envisioned and implemented, along with new methods of nego-tiating peace among warring nations and cultures. Solutions always come when human thinking gets elevated and expanded. Our world will heal more quickly when each of us embraces the point of view of a hybrid vigor, in everyone's own special unique way. Spiritually evolving, right now, is the solution to all our earthly woes. Dropping previously-held, antiquated modes of thinking and being, ones that just don't work anymore, is the new paradigm shift represented by we hybrid vigors.

Let's be real: our species' future is threatened. The planet can self-repair itself, as it has many times before this modern-day environmental crisis. Reversing the extinction of homo sapiens depends on us—each one of us hybrid vigors—to stop the trend of humankind's being stupid! It's time to change. A sea change happens when each of us pays attention to every epiphany we encounter, and keeps trying to make things better, no matter what.

Historically, creative worldwide breakthroughs have happened, simultaneously. It's as if a synchronistic spark around the globe gets set off, like an alarm goes off at the same time in everyone's DNA. Evolution *It*-self is part of our human species' collective unconscious. This tendency of similar discoveries has happened many times before in recorded history. How ironic that far-flung cultures have such similar folk tales. And seemingly serendipitous innovations that occur to non-communicating individuals in faraway places, are more common than seem feasible. Take the case of Edison and Tesla both working to harness electricity. Game-changing scientific breakthroughs often happen in the same manner in which ancient myths arose. In nearly identical fashion, but in far separate, vastly different cultures completely isolated from each other, a similar insight into human nature suddenly appears. Current solutions to our world's many challenges will announce themselves in the same way, to open-minded individuals who are actively seeking answers to the questions of our survival.

This phenomenon, simultaneously finding solutions to whatever challenges are at hand, happens naturally whenever civilization is ready to take the next huge leap in our collective experience. Exactly as it did most recently when a sweeping transformation of the world happened via the digital age. And before that, upon the advent of the industrial age ... and before that, the agricultural age.

Each of us has all the tools needed for our survival and to help heal our entire planet. We are conscious beings. At this moment in time there are among us extraordinary geniuses and ordinary folk alike, who are awakening to their hybrid vigor-ness. Everyday more folks are becoming aware that materialism is not the solution for happiness. Many of us have found great pleasure and fulfillment from journeying inward, discovering the stillness of a peaceful mind. Besides the current (and gratefully necessary) worldwide popularity of yoga, meditation and other mindful practices, awakened people are undergoing personal transformations in astounding numbers. This inspires even more tidal waves of people to become interested in developing higher consciousness. We have already reached unprecedented numbers of born-awakened souls—the so-called *Indigo Children*, the modern name given for enlightened-at-birth humans, which has been happening all over the globe in unprecedented numbers for several decades now. Spontaneous awakening is the natural result of this collective shift in human consciousness we are currently living through, right now. The spiritual awakening of our human family is in full process. There is no more waiting for the shift to happen. The domino effect of this next step in human evolution that we are in *right now* has been observed and commented on here already.

Right now we are in the midst of the consciousness transition of ordinary homo sapiens into the more elevated subspecies of hybrid vigors. When enough of us proclaim our commitment, as proof of the permanent level of evolution we've already reached, as a species, perhaps a conclave of worldwide biologists will agree that it's time for our millennium-old species to deserve a new nomen-clature.

And then, the age of *homo spiritus* will perhaps officially begin.

Until that time, however, the transformation of humankind's consciousness continues in ever-increasing ripples of positive change throughout our precious home, planet Earth.

Humans are spontaneously being awakened by the over-whelming number of hybrid vigors surrounding them. We are impressive in our numbers, we folks who have already freed our dormant craving for a more meaningful *spiritual* life. We are folks of all colors, creeds, and cultures who are nourishing this yearning, alongside pursuing physical desires and intellectual curiosities. This sea change of humanity is the reality of the here and now. Our human species is in the midst of an evolutionary watershed moment, one that is precipitated, firstly, by the recognition of each of us having learned to love our own Self, our tuned-to-Nature, true Self.

A huge *waterfall of energy* is bursting upon each one of us, changing the way we think, awakening people to be hybrid vigors in remarkable, unprecedented numbers. This surge of needing-to-change won't stop until the majority of us have been awakened, one person at a time. Solutions, inventions, new ways of being, will arise spontaneously and simultaneously, as if an inner alarm bell has gone off, synchronistically, in every person's inner sanctum, minds and hearts, facilitating the re-birth of our human species. Right now, we HVs are in all nations, acting as seedlings for our future blended family of humankind. We love and care for each another, without any need for separation of any kind; without animosity, without needing to control or be controlled by one another. Greater things await humankind. The archaic ways, mundane bickering over borders, cultural differences, religious preferences, aesthetics, are becoming ineffective, and eventually will be obsolete. Those are societal aspects of the juvenile stage of humankind, emblematic of the wasteful control issues that have obsessed our species for far too long.

One by one, we will find our own inner Self going over what I can only describe, and name, from my own experience—the all-powerful Waterfall of Life. Its waters anoint us in *Spontaneous and Joyful Change*. The particular catalyst for my having been pushed over the edge of this life-altering Waterfall, this psychic shock, was the spiritual dis-ease of Self-destructive addiction. Other folks might get pushed over the Waterfall's edge, forced into changing themselves due to other types of personal crises. Such things as hair-pulling politics, paralyzing fear of a next massacre, domestic or terrorist-related, or some other tragedy occurring, real or imagined, hurtles a lot of folks over the edge of this imaginary waterfall I'm painting for you. All these, understandably, are drastic factors that provide a person the *impetus of change*, the headwaters of this Waterfall to which I refer. Each crisis that arises provides—like any unexpected and dangerous waterfall or rapids each of us is forced to ride over when it pops up on the River of Life—a next set of answers for a person's ability to easily resolve seemingly irresolvable dilemmas.

All answers lie in the realm of a hybrid vigor's newly opened, all-embracing approach to what this life here on Earth, is all about. Radical, never before dreamed of, reasonable and functional solutions for all of life's enigmas, is already underway, full throttle, right now. The time is ripe for a serious spotlight to shine upon the darkness of denial that keeps obvious solutions obscured from our collective awareness.

Hope never goes unnoticed by the Unseens.

People who are receptive, receive. People who have closed themselves off to possibilities, are sentenced to repeat old mistakes. These unfortunate, hard-hearted types, either wither in dis-ease or live their lives half-awake, like automatons ... never questioning whether they are happy or not, never realizing they have the power to change right at their fingertips.

A solution to any one of life's many challenges is as close as paying attention to, for instance, a dream, choosing to think positively, remembering to plant seeds of positive thought instead of promoting negativity. And, most importantly, remembering to follow our bliss.

Today, after learning to listen to my inner Voice—the one each of us potential hybrid vigors has within us, our own higher Self's inner-direction Voice—I know the only challenge there is, is to stay focused on Love. No matter what.

Every fairy tale, every legend, every pagan deity and each of the Great Religions of the World was invented to pass on to others some earth-shaking, sometimes scary or unbelievable tidbit of information, in an entertaining, easy-to-remember story form. Parables are easier to remember than a dull set of to-do rules. Edge-of-seat engaging stories, Isis and Osiris and Horus, Aesop's fables, Thor and his thunderbolt, Siegfried and the Valkyries, Diana of the forest, Apollo and Daphne—all these are methods of passing along the wonders of humankind's eternal search for Love, especially Self Love: finding the faith, the *belief in*, of something much greater than our own little self.

The story I'm telling you now is no different. Sooner or later, each and every one of us will meet the situation that literally or figuratively, tosses us over a cataclysmic, life-altering game-changing Waterfall of Life. For the storyline's purpose in this rumination of mine, let's call this particularly awesome fairy tale waterfall of mine, the formidable name of …

"The Abyss of Perceived Human Potential—the Unlimited Version."

Do I hear you chuckling?

When you get your first glimpse of this astounding Waterfall of Life, whether in a deep meditation session, an *aha!* moment catalyzed by a personal insight—sparked by something, a book, a painting, a song, an inspiring teacher—believe me, you'll know it when it happens. This is called a *spiritual awakening*. To whatever degree one finds themself *in the game-change*, your first pitch, or the final grand slam—is of little consequence.

When it happens (if it hasn't already) you'll want to feel as comfortable in that human skin of yours as possible. Because a pure spiritual energy force wearing a human bodysuit is what you are, and always have been. Remembering this will delight you beyond any pleasure you've ever known. To awaken to this plain-as-day, yet hidden-to-many Truth is your birthright to realize—at your own time and pace—simply because you've been born as a human being.

The good news is, you get to choose whether you want enlightenment fast (here and now) or in safe, easy-to-digest increments. You get everything you need to awaken from whatever dramatically intense *inner* experience (remember: going over Waterfalls of Life is an *inside job!*) or—you will find yourself repeatedly recognizing the uncomfortable pain of not knowing who and what you are, over and over. You will meet one Waterfall after the next, until … you … surrender … and begin to remember.

How do I know this? It's my story and it's millions of other awakened souls' story. I've heard many who have described in detail, about the process of rising above their lower self. I've also witnessed the uncomfortable effect, what happens to people who are not willing to accept our human Divinity, this magical state of our Beingness. Most poignantly I saw this when I attended Mom's last months, weeks, and days' worth of her fear of dying. Fearless in life, Mom's passing was agony to witness, up to her last tormented breath. Eve's was opposite to my father Linwood's final passage, at which I was also honored to have privately, solely assisted him.

My father's passing from human to, once again, pure Spirit form, as I have earlier recounted, gifted me the proof I'd always wished for, believing as strongly as I always did in the consciousness of Love being the uniting energy of all Life *It-self.*

One day after safely landing, not crashing over the latest of the uproarious waterfalls my seeking path has sent me over, I awoke to finally realize (am I more stubborn than the average person?) that I had to change, or—I would die. I had no idea I'd wake up that day—after my father's death when I was hurled over my *believe-or-perish Waterfall of Life*—as a hybrid-vigor wannabe. By sharing the twists and turns of my story with you, I hope you will join me, and the uncountable numbers of already-awakened hybrid vigors who've come before us in human history.

All it takes to become a hybrid vigor kind of person is to make the conscious choice—and never hide from or deny our true nature of unconditional Love ever again.

For every challenge to humanity, remedies lie within each of us who allows our Self to embrace and work with our own Light within. Recognizing this possibility is the true meaning of the Eastern greeting: Namaste, "My Light within recognizes yours, and we are equal." The Light of consciousness is the Source of creativity. That's why I love to linger in its titillating atmosphere each time I tune into my breath, for even just a moment if that's all I have.

The Light within all of us is the Life Force, pure consciousness *It*-self.

The next step, for any who are intrigued about becoming a hybrid vigor, is directed by how well you can relax and trust, listen, and do—what you're inspired to do—from the Mystery Source within. Learn to listen to your Unseen's guiding Voice that comes from within each of us.

When we allow, and then follow our own inner guidance, it's like trusting an inner compass that gives direction to all of creation. This is how hybrid vigor humans operate. We trust Spirit.

There's no difference between the world's dilemmas and our own private ones. The macrocosm is the same as the microcosm.

"What we do to Earth, our Mother Earth, we do to ourselves," stated the Native American elder, Chief Seattle to the invading white men back in the nineteenth century. "Life is a continuous web. Everything is interconnected."

Many believe, as I do, that today, the early twenty-first century, is the tipping-point of this upward consciousness shift, long predicted by various belief systems. As we've seen, this shift of awakening humans has already been reached. There's nothing stopping this sea change we're in. Many of us citizens of Earth are trying harder than ever to learn from our mistakes, despite naysayers' objections. Thanks to the internet's speed, we lift our voices higher, louder, together—some of us demonstrating, tweeting or obsessively posting positive thoughts and inspirations; others arting, singing, inventing or following our bliss in science, technology, and other new fields that spring up from today's emerging needs, healing yesterday's wounds. Inspired and enthused by the spiritual transformation happening all around us—hybrid vigors everywhere are facilitating the evolution of our human race *Right Now!*

Citizens of all nations must now insist on electing enlightened (open-minded, open-hearted) leaders to take over navigating the prows of our world's super-powers; replacing antiquated, controlling leaders with inspired hybrid vigors. New, open-minded leaders at the helm to guide our world countries, like giant ships gracefully and harmoniously maneuvering in the Sea Change of Life on Earth, we steer toward the future. Each ship steers through dangerously charged, generations-long dilemmas, stalemates, old cultural scars and tendencies, toward the Light of transformation.

Proclaiming to be a hybrid vigor means you are participating in the new, consciously-heightened Self-born-species of humankind. *Think* you are now more highly evolved, consciously, spiritually— and you already *are*. Think yourself awakened to higher states of Being, and you *are*.

Your breath-watching focus becomes your sidekick, your handy mindful-tool, a convenient quickie reminder of Presence— the state of focused awareness. Your breath is your best friend and your most trusted, ethical Teacher of all.

Our entire world is becoming positively influenced with hybrid vigors in every sector, as we learn to compassionately settle our differences and solve the intricate challenges of modern life with the unlimited power of our newly elevated abilities.

One individual influences all those around them, their acquaintances, their inner circle, their social tribe, their family and coworkers ... their company's boss ... their country's politics. This is how the ripple effect that we are in works. There's no stopping humanity's forward evolution!

Every action begins with the seed of a thought. Watch Your Self! Watch and safeguard your thinking to *be positive*. Correct any negatives as they arise.

A single blended family, however small, is the same, in microcosm, as the macrocosm of our entire blended worldwide family of humankind.

Each of us—from any particular walk of life—is a member of the global Earth family. It doesn't kill anyone of us to go over an imaginary waterfall of creative blue-sky thinking now and then, to let more thoughts of expanded awareness become our normal way of thinking. That's what we're doing here. We're practicing spiritual evolution. We're pumping up our spiritual muscles by thinking these cool, do-able thoughts, together. Please remember this Truth: it's good to fake it till you make it. *Pretend* you're a hybrid vigor, and … you *are* one! This method works like *a charm*.

My job, as a writer who arts, is to help us all to remember, now that I've remembered who and what *I am*.

I am … and yes, in plural form, *we are* … *Oneness*.

As we ride the Waterfall's next hurtling, phantasmagoric energy wave of Life—tripping us, sliding us forward, screaming at us, kicking some of us over the falls, or in the ass if we balk—we'll still get flung over the next slippery slope on our journey along this incredibly exciting evolutionary path we're on together, here and now.

CHAPTER 13

who are we, really?

Ferociously protective, yet cuddly cute in its teddy-bear incarnation, a bear—brown, white, black, and all shades in between—is a major totem animal of Native Americans. Along with the great blue heron (*air*) and dolphin (*water*), bear (*earth*) is one of my protectors, as much or more, than my own Unseen, whom I fondly call *Noname*.

Ever since becoming a ritualized blood sister in childhood to my Iroquois girlfriend Bernice, I have been discovering just how much of a protector the bear is to me.

All who wish to, may call upon and use Bear as a symbol of great inner and outer strength.

The bear awakens each spring from its long slumber, hibernation being more of a twilight zone than a complete state of unconsciousness. So too, each person who wishes to awaken from their own slumber can remember themselves as a big strong bear whose personal *daily* habit is—*to awaken*.

Mother bears will kill to protect their young, as many species do when provoked. Surely, a bear-mother's ferocity is heart-stoppingly frightful for any to witness.

When feeling under attack, whether it's your freedom or your actual life, close your eyes and ask the *bear within you*, the spirit of Bear, to rise up and show you how to keep the balance of a threatened existence more honestly, more forthrightly, more ... animal-like.

We must always remember our ancestral roots, never forgetting that we human animals are mammals. We may have superior rational thinking, and yes, we have *spoken* language ... but aside from those two more refined attributes, there's little to differentiate us from many of our thinking, feeling animal brothers and sisters.

Whenever troubled or feeling low, depressed or fearful, this is a good time to call upon the totem of Bear. I always feel protected, encouraged and strengthened by asking Bear to come be at my side, as a symbolically magical support during difficult times.

Whenever our perceptions become inured to *too much*—too much violence, too much materialism, too much stimulus from screens, too much negativity—ask Bear to awaken us from our slumber. Because an elevated Bear-like way of being is similar to seeing outstretched golden plains of springtime awakening below, from atop a cloud-kissing mountaintop, within which our sleeping cave of forgetfulness lays hidden. Look all around, once awakened. Our hybrid-vigor selves get a much clearer picture of *how things are* from this up-high vantage point, much better than we did from our old perspective, down below the heights of expanded understanding, which is available to any who wish *It*.

An awakened mind is the same as the symbolic awakening that Bear performs each spring, invigorating its purpose for Being.

Ask Bear to surround any situation that confounds, protecting us with its comforting largesse. Ask Bear to share some of its fearlessness whenever a bolster of courage is needed.

One may not be sent as a representative to the U.N., but the character of Bear within us can be counted on to protect what's important when our feelings get provoked.

Leading up to an escalating confrontation, increasing numbers of demonstrators were gathering to protest outside my town's quietly devout Islamic Center out on busy Route 207. A member of Unity and Peace, a local pro-active peace-making group in our community, was commuting to work on Monday, July 20, a solid year before the tumultuous 2016 election, when this woman happened to pass the mosque.

She noticed a group of angry, American flag-waving demonstrators who numbered in the dozens. On subsequent days, whenever passing the mosque, she noticed the number of anti-Islam demonstrators kept increasing. In a few days it would be Friday, the Islamic holy day of worship, when devoted families with children were expected to arrive at the mosque.

The commuting woman had by now texted other Unity and Peace friends, who then sent out emails to the leaders of the local Charter for Compassion, a worldwide web-driven net of concerned and committed citizens who strive to live by the Golden Rule. Many of the members of that local group who were reached that day swung into action.

Having specialized in being a volunteer go-between, this protective, Bear-like silver-haired woman, who for years had volunteered to help settle disputes as a professional mediator, stepped up to take action. The mediator called an Islamic lady she knew to ask if she and her fellow Muslims who worshipped at the mosque each Friday would like some help.

"I'm experienced in this sort of thing," the mediator said. "I'll help you sort out whatever problem is causing the demonstrators to keep appearing—obviously they're angry—waving their American flags and making all that commotion."

"Most definitely," the Muslim woman replied. "Thanks, we need your help."

Outside the small orthodox Islamic Center, T-shirted, baseball-capped folks who drove oversized pickups and hid their licensed guns and rifles under front seats, continued to be incensed. Their shouts of anti-Islamic sentiments grew more aggressive each day. For a second Friday, demonstrators continued to block the way of the mosque's worshippers, intimidating the innocent devout folks who wore different clothes than they, ate different food, and called God by a different, Arabic, name than they did. Outside the large mosque compound, Stars-and-Stripes flag-waving agitators became more incensed after that week's latest national tragedy occurred.

Another heinous attack had been perpetrated. This one by an American military man named Muhammad, who senselessly killed five fellow servicemen in Chattanooga. Up to this point, in my town, it had been a rather small pack of working-class American men and women who were shouting angry words and waving big flags. After the Tennessee event, the local protestors and signs tripled outside the mosque, demonstrating on the sidewalk running alongside one of the major thoroughfares into town. Insufficient, softly-spoken words from intimidated Muslim men as they turned into the mosque's private driveway, as they took their panicked families to worship on the Friday after this latest unfortunate massacre, only increased the demonstrators' machismo. No one among the Muslim men knew how to deal with such an agitated crowd. Much less negotiate peacefully with angry southern white folks who looked like they had itchy trigger fingers, along with big shiny Confederate belt buckles, and mini-flags sewed onto denim hunting vests.

The mosque community was now terrified, for good reason, rightfully fearing for their lives. The Islamic woman desperately texted her mediator friend in the Peace and Unity group, who relayed the cry for help to others in the local *CharterFor-Compassion.org* bunch. That next Friday's gathering at the mosque, would be what the Islamic woman feared, and what she described to her mediator friend as "A showdown between them and us."

Meanwhile, the leader of the street demonstrators, a Facebook instigator it'd soon be found out, was putting things up on her news-feed, purposefully to agitate others, trying to rally people across the county and beyond. This *protestor-lady* claimed suspicions of our small town's Muslims spreading anti-American propaganda. Misinformed statements about "other Muslim attacks like Chattanooga" appeared, including, incongruously, the most recent and senseless gunning of members of the unsuspecting African-American prayer group meeting in South Carolina, nine folks who were ruthlessly slain by a disturbed young white man who'd joined them, ostensibly to pray. A tragedy not in the slightest bit related to religious observance of Islam, but a racial attack perpetrated by a gun-toting, disturbed individual who, truthfully, was a domestic terrorist, and likely, a white supremacist.

Then, an even more alarming post was seen on the Facebook feed of the demonstrators' local leader. It read: "We plan on being here *(the mosque, that upcoming Friday)* until they show who they really are—terrorists, and then we'll be ready to take them out!"

Then, somehow, nobody knows *exactly how*, an email from the volunteer mediator's private account, the woman who had *privately* offered to help the Islamic community settle the hair-raising, now weeks-long dispute, was put up on the demonstrators' Facebook page! An act of sneaky hacking no one to this day has been able to figure how it happened. This serious invasion of privacy did its job, however, of scaring the good-hearted, white-haired mediator. Not enough, apparently, to keep this kind Bear-like protector from trying to help solve the Islamic Center's escalating crisis.

Appalled that her private correspondence had been stolen, the mediator immediately sent out another e-request for members of the local chapters of Unity and Peace, and the Compassion Group, and any other sympathetic folks in town, secular or religious, to meet that Friday to help support the rights of these devoted Muslim men, women and children to worship at their Center.

At the end of that email asking for solidarity in these efforts, the silver-haired mediator sweetly added, "We'll bring enough chocolate cake and lemonade for all our good neighbors."

Soon enough, a rebuttal post appeared on the protestor-lady's Facebook page. How they'd show up with BLTs, it read, enough for a hundred people, saying that "Bacon would taste especially good there at the mosque," a cruel dig at the orthodox Muslim's dietary restrictions.

Then our local paper got wind of the coming face-off.

On Thursday, it boldly placed on the front page, above all other headlines, an article that horrified everyone's sense of common decency. It was meant to be newsworthy but had the opposite effect of pouring gasoline onto an already raging fire.

Illustrating the news item of the ongoing clash between the mosque and demonstrators was a close-up photo of two red-hot angry-faced overweight women holding up a sign that read: "Islam is of the Devil, 666."

Seeing that front page write-up, I decided to interrupt my work project and join this humane effort the next day, Friday. I wanted to stand among the growing group of anti-demonstrators, because word was spreading in our officially designated *Compassionate Town*, that bodies were needed "to show up in support of our Muslim neighbors, tomorrow, the Islamic holy day. We must protect our neighbors so they may enter their mosque without an altercation," the email I received from the white-haired mediator read.

The next day, all the flag-flying demonstrators' bacon-lettuce-tomato sandwiches would go bad because only six protestors showed up. Perhaps due to the unflattering-to-the-protestors photos and embarrassing front-page article our local paper had printed.

Our group, the anti-demonstrators, had over sixty souls who stood together in the humid heat of that early sunny morning of July 24. Quietly, without signs, without shouts or malice of any kind, we men and women of all sorts, some with religious persuasions and others with just a strong belief in common decency, showed up to express our empathy with the Islamic group. We stood along the long driveway entrance, from the main road all the way to the mosque entrance a hundred yards away, showing our protection of theirs, ours, and all citizens' constitutional rights, considered our greatest privilege here in the democracy of America. Most essentially is the freedom that allows all Americans to worship as they choose, which was the founding basis for protecting the rights of all newly arrived peoples in the New World that our forebears from the Old World were designing, in what became the Constitution of the U.S.A.

We anti-demonstrators came by the carloads, to protect our neighbors from any more religious harassment. As soon as we arrived, our group was invited to join the Islamic community inside for prayer, men sitting with men, women with women.

Because of the wisdom of protective Bear that manifested within the white-haired mediator, she negotiated a peaceful resolution, thanks in part to our anti-demonstrators' respectful, yet insistently strong show of support.

Perhaps the anti-Islamic protestors, the expected crowd that was meant to eat those mean BLTs, failed to show because they finally remembered our country's founding tradition of welcoming all, no matter if a person worshipped God or a tree, or which of the *Thousand Names for the Almighty* people might use, or how a person claims their belief, or non-belief, to be. Perhaps the angry mob, reduced to only a handful at this final show-down, remembered America's Founding Fathers' principles of religious freedom. Or maybe the protestors could finally see how they'd grown so fearful of America's newest wave of foreigners, people different-than themselves, these *others* who were, in effect, no different than the many generations of others who'd come before them, seeking America's freedoms. Maybe they'd decided to relax and let these Muslim-*others* become just plain American immigrants, just like waves of Irish, Chinese, Germans, and Jews and many other immigrants had before them; these demonstrators' parents or grandparents or however many generations back it went, when *their forebears* first arrived here.

Outside the mosque's fenced-off gate, the six lone demonstrators paced the sidewalk, waving their over-sized flags and shouting futilely at passing cars. None of the angry half-dozen were in any mood for sharing the cake or lemonade offered them. Only after the mediator began quietly discussing with the angry six, did they begin to acknowledge that the Muslims—some had been American citizens for decades—held the same constitutional rights that the protestors themselves did.

Right after I arrived, I ran into the friendly man whom my family has known for over thirty years.

"Hey, Tony, what are you doing here?" I called out to him, wondering why he was dressed like that.

I was used to seeing him in his Tony's Pizza shop, wearing work pants and a collared shirt. I was wondering why he was wearing that floor-length robe just as the white-haired mediator, who stood alongside me in our protestors' line, pointed out that he, my good friend Tony, was the lay leader of the Islamic community. "He volunteered to lead his group, since they don't have funds enough to bring in a *real Imam*," she quietly added.

That stopped me in my tracks. Tony was smiling and waving back at me so I walked over to him and greeted the Middle Eastern-looking man with a full beard who was dressed like I'd never seen him before, in a long white robe and skullcap.

He was the owner of Mom's favorite Italian joint, where she'd been taking her family for the past couple decades to eat his incredibly delicious white pizza. "Tony's got the best flavored sauce, the best crust," Mom told anyone who listened.

"He's from someplace like Lebanon or Algeria, I'm not sure which," Mom whispered to me once as we waited for our mouth-watering mozzarella, parmesan and ricotta pizza to cook. "I asked him where he's from once, but I forget," she giggled without a care. Mom loved Tony, and that was all I needed to know.

As the years went by I silently wondered what that dark spot could be that I noticed beginning to appear in the middle of Tony's forehead, and how it seemed to become more pronounced with each next year's white pizza I'd share with my parents on my not-too-often visits to their Florida home, in the years before I moved there too.

"Does he put ashes on, like an Ash Wednesday thing, between his eyebrows," I finally asked Mom.

"No," Eve whispered back, "I asked him that once myself. That dark spot is from Tony bowing his head to the floor during his prayers, which he told me he does many times throughout the day. That's a prayer-bruise, honey. Now hush up, Linduta, stop staring and let's eat!"

Over the years, whenever we visited his hidden-away spot, I knew that Tony was as un-Italian as the Korans he had on display, offering them freely to anyone who was interested ever since 9/11. It was obvious even before that sad date, though, that Tony's dark skin wasn't of Latin origin. Even those who didn't speak with Tony could figure that out, by spying the painted desert scenes of hillsides filled with Lebanese cedars with which he decorated his restaurant's walls. And noted the framed photographs of gilded Arabic script all around, as prominently displayed as the American flag he flew, somewhat oddly, right over the Coke machine.

Tony and I greeted each other familiarly. I looked into my friend's thickly-lashed, twinkling brown eyes after we hugged. His generous smile was the same as every time I'd seen him before, even though this was the first time I'd ever seen him outside of his pizza shop. The first time I'd seen him wearing a skullcap and loose white robe instead of his regular dark work clothes.

"So, your name really isn't Tony, right?" I softly said.

He laughed, the same old merry sound, filled with the same kind of good-natured fun.

He shook his head and white teeth flashed as he laughed. I could tell he was tickled. That it took me this long and under these peculiar circumstances to finally ask his real name. He acted as if this were a delightful joke, his letting me think he had an Italian name all these years, never correcting anyone when they, of course, naturally, called him Tony.

"No, I'm Yusef!" he chuckled in an even brighter tone. "I told your mother that a long time ago but she never remembers. She always calls me Tony, and I'm happy to be Tony. Call me anything you like," he said with a brilliant grin in front of my companions, the staring, wondering anti-demonstrators, as we stood before them in the middle of the driveway.

Suddenly I felt self-conscious. I didn't know if it was against his religion for Tony, or Yusef rather, to hug a woman, as he'd just done. Mom always had greeted him, her special pizza-man, with a big hug. But now I knew he was the Imam; okay, the temporary layman one at his mosque. Still, an Imam is an Imam: a man of leadership and respect. I wanted to acknowledge that dignified position to my friend in front of his and my peers.

I have to admit, at the time I didn't know any particulars about Islam, other than those archaic head scarves and burqas we feminists cringe over. I'd never read a single portion of the Koran, and never had met anyone who practiced Islam, except for the man who stood before me now. I made a silent promise to myself to call him Yusef from then on, and would insist other members of my family did as well.

He, the cloaked Imam brought his attention back to the nearby volunteer mediator, the non-Muslim, snow-haired, bear-like momma protector, if there ever was one. "You'll have to excuse me," Yusef winked at me. "Duty calls."

He turned and went with the mediator to the gate entrance. With her encouragement and coaching, a few minutes later he said in a newly emboldened voice to the protestors, "Hello friends! I am the Imam here, the one in charge. May I invite all you folks who seem to be unhappy about something, to come inside the mosque, if you wish. Come and join us as we worship. Come inside to see what kind of people we are, to hear what our prayers are like. We want you to see for yourselves what's going on inside our place, here."

There was a loud mumbling among the few protestors. Then they came closer. They dropped to eye level their wood staffs with the high-held flags. The group's spokesperson, the Facebook instigator, came forward and began to speak quietly with Yusef and the teddy-bear of a mediator.

The protestors would not join the prayers going on inside. Later, I'd find out why.

The leader, the woman of angry Facebook posts, told Yusef and the mediator that, "We never go nowhere we can't take our weapons."

Before the two sides had met, the sheriff's deputy discreetly informed the mediator and Yusef that "The protestors are carrying and have permits for their concealed weapons. I've checked. They're legal."

When the mediator mentioned in her sweet-as-sugar tone to the protestor-lady that the mosque was a weapons-free zone, the leader said her group wouldn't go anywhere they "couldn't exercise our right to bear firearms, our due rights," as the dour-faced woman put it.

Then the skillful mediator began a conversation between Yusef and the protestors, out at the entrance gate. While our swarm of anti-demonstrators watched in the hot sun, the now-arriving Muslim worshipping families were able to enter the mosque without interference.

After a few minutes of quietly talking: the leader of the protestors, the white-haired mediator, and white-robed Yusef, broke apart. Straight away, Yusef joined his congregation in the mosque while the mediator came over to explain to our anti-demonstrating group what had just happened.

"That protestor-lady," the mediator's honey-flavored drawl began, "told Yusef and me that their real beef was because the Islamic Center isn't flying the American flag outside. So, as Imam,

Yusef told her, 'We'll be happy to fly the Stars and Stripes, no problem! Why didn't anyone just ask us before?'

"After he said Okay, that was that. She cooled down," the mediator said, "as if nothing had ever happened. Everything got settled in five minutes flat."

One last kick had to happen, though; that's the usual way human nature, and Nature Herself goes, right? To end this otherwise successful interchange on an unexpected note, one which no one but who reads this will ever find out about. The next day, instead of the easy solution agreed upon on Friday by Yusef and the leader of the protestors, who insisted their only gripe was for the U.S. flag to be flown visibly outside the mosque—this troublesome woman managed to cause more unnecessary aggravation. She showed up at the appointed hour, and more head scratching resulted.

The mediator—who came on Saturday to support Yusef—later privately relayed to me the bizarre scene that followed.

"Can you believe it?" the mediator told me in a hush-hush tone. "Right after they purchased it at Walmart the protestor-lady altered that brand-new flag! What wickedness! The nerve! And then, making like she was all high and mighty, presenting it to the mosque herself, pretending like it was some goodwill kind of gift, imagine!

"I noticed it even before it got hoisted up," the mediator reported. "That the flag they presented to Yusef had been altered, in a way that might not be so obvious. If I hadn't shown up, Yusef and his people would have been duped! That nasty lady was trying to force the mosque to fly our flag upside down, in absolute total disrespect! The way it was rigged, it could only fly upside down, with its grommets moved like they'd been. Imagine doing such a thing to poor unsuspecting immigrants. Even though Yusef had an American flag displayed at his pizza shop (the mediator too, was a fan of Tony's cozy restaurant), he would never have suspected that people could do something so … so low and conniving as what that gal tried to do to him and the Islamic folks.

"If I hadn't been there, Yusef probably would never have suspected. Such deviance, I'm appalled!" the sweet-as-vinegar mediator fumed, who'd spent decades with her minister-husband helping to arbitrate difficult people-conflicts. "As soon as poor Yusef started to put this upside-down flag on the pole's rope, I yelled *Stop!*

"Wait a minute! I yelled. Wait a dang-gong minute!" the mediator boomed as she retold me her surprise exchange. "What's going on?" she continued, "I asked that protestor-lady and her cohort. Then I told them in no uncertain terms: I see how you put these new grommets on the wrong side, on purpose. You're trying to aggravate things, aren't you? Shame on you!"

The mediator continued explaining to me. "What do you mean? the protest leader-lady shot back at me, pretending she was innocent. 'We're doing what's right, for this situation,' she said to me with a sneaky attitude that was totally uncalled for.

"Who gave you the authority to tamper with the way the United States flag flies, I asked her. This flag of yours is rigged, I told her straight up! You'd better have a good explanation why."

The mediator, in her excited, exaggerated state, was relating this bizarre exchange between her and the protest-lady for my behalf alone. There was no one else present that day when she told me this in confidence.

As she was telling me this moronic twist of the mosque conflict, I got chills up my spine. Looking at this demure mediator-woman's protective Bear-stance, hearing her Roar against Injustice like she'd done, like she will again, many times over, I felt such pride in this person who so beautifully, so easily owned her own power, standing right before me. This woman, I knew—like many of us, men and women who are in touch with our protective feminine power, our *Bear* within—she'd never take shit *from anyone!*

The mediator was jumping from one foot to another as she continued telling me what happened.

"I waited for the protestor-lady to explain. Yusef stood by my side, completely taken aback, speechless that such a thing was happening. He never even suspected that an upside-down flag could be anything more than an hapless mistake, or a manufacturing glitch. He was way-too trusting that this lady was a do-gooder, to suspect her pulling a trick on him. If I hadn't been there, would he ever have even noticed the flag being different? Probably not. Heck, I practically didn't, but I'm more suspecting than he is. And I knew that protestor-lady was the one who'd done the outrageous hacking of my email, before this, so I didn't trust her one iota.

"So I told her, 'It's plain to see the grommets have been intentionally moved. The old ones have been hemmed over, see here, so nobody could notice them,' I said to her, pointing to the flag's bulging, hastily sewn hem. That lady must think everybody except her is stupid.

"She admitted it. Then she told me then, 'Okay. We did it on purpose. Because the code book says it's a special sign of respect to fly it upside down.'

"What kind of respect? I asked her.

"She said, 'It signifies that American soldiers have been killed in the line of duty.'

"What? I said right back at her. If that's true I don't know, but it doesn't sound right, ma'am."

The whole time the mediator was telling me her side of the story, I couldn't believe how courteous she had been during that Saturday's confrontation. Me? Much as I would love to say I saw the Divine in her protesting adversary that day, I pretty much can guarantee you I would have wanted to bitch-slap that nasty lady by that point, sure thing, or have gotten mouthy on her, at least. My mediator friend is a saint, and surely a better HV than I, I thought, as I listened to her continue telling me what transpired next.

"So, I asked the protestor-lady, 'Just where do you see any soldiers killed around here?'

"Not here! she had the nerve to screech at me like a cat ready to pounce. Then she screamed, 'At the towers! In Iraq, in Afghanistan!

Lots of our boys killed over there!' That rough woman yelled at me, as if I weren't just as upset as anyone, my own self, with the endless casualties in this never-ending war on terrorism."

Here, the mediator stopped recounting that strange discourse for a second or two, stood shaking her head in utter disgust, before she continued.

"This must be your idea of some sick joke, I said, putting it right back on her. Lady, I said, no one knows what an upside-down flag means, nobody! I certainly didn't, until you said just now what the code is. Which doesn't sound right to me. So you can bet I'm going to look it up when I get home. An ordinary car driving by seeing our flag like that wouldn't understand any of what you're saying, I told her.

"Then I toned it way down," Bear-Human said. "But I was still red-hot mad, let me tell you. By flying this flag, I told her real quiet-like, in this way, upside down like that, that just seems alarming, and real harsh treatment of these nice Islamic folks here, who've agreed to do what your group demanded. It's disrespectful to the Muslims, on whose property the flag is flying. And it's disrespectful to the people who've died in this terrible conflict, who haven't got anything to do with this itty-bitty argument going on here between your group and this small prayerful congregation of our tiny town's Muslims. Am I right?"

The mediator shook her silver head in frustration re-enacting the scene for me. She took a deep breath, and tried to settle down her riled-up emotions before telling me what happened next.

"I told that protestor-lady," my friend said, "I insist you take that flag back you gave Yusef.

"Then I dove into my tote and brought out the flag I'd brought, *Just In Case*. In case somebody had forgotten to bring one, I mean.

"Never did I think, not once! that someone would stoop so low as to alter a flag's grommets, and pull such a dirty trick on such unsuspecting folks like that gal tried to do. The average American doesn't know proper flag etiquette!

"So Yusef and I traded the upside down one for the proper one I'd brought, and, without a word, we hoisted it high and real proudly.

"Then I took a picture of that standard regulation flag flying outside the Islamic Center, and asked the protest leader for her email address.

"I'm sending this to you, I told her. For you to kindly post on your Facebook page. And the next time you have a problem about the center here, you can write me personally and I'll do my best to help make you happy. Let's call off any further demonstrations, shall we?

"The woman nodded to me, and without a word more scribbled her email address in my notebook, and that was that," my friend ended with a satisfied smile.

The white-haired Bear-woman told me that Yusef never mentioned to anyone (but I will here) that there were no U.S. flags flying outside any Catholic, Protestant, Baptist or Fundamentalist Church in our village at that time, nor our Jewish synagogue, neither the Buddhist nor Hindu temple, nor the Unitarian Universalist, nor the Baha'i Group or the Center for Spiritual Living that I or anyone ever noticed. And nobody ever demanded they had to do so, either.

Because in America, church and state are supposed to be separate. But the Imam, an amiable prayerful man who has flown the American flag over the soda dispenser at his pizza joint since I first met him three decades before, Yusef agreed to this preposterous demand—in the name of wanting to make peace. And peace was made, even though the humble Imam sweetly agreed to do what a lot of religious leaders in America balk at—being asked to mix up an outer national allegiance with their expressions of faith in the Almighty.

CHAPTER 14

sinners and saints, skunks and stingrays

From my immigrant-farmer grandmother I'd learned early on, that the only way to wash away a skunk's nasty smell, once it sprayed you—was to squish a plump, red ripe tomato and use it instead of soap and water to neutralize the animal's repulsive stench. "That get smell out of clothes," Grammom Antonina said, "otherwise, have to bury them."

Still, whenever I detected that distinctive malodor, whether just a quick whiff as my parents drove their Oldsmobile down a winding country road, or later as a woman, I sped down a highway with the hot wind blowing in my face from another opened window, the lingering wafts of skunk sneaking in with the breeze caused, I admit, a pleasant sensation that even today sets off memory links that light up my brain's receptors with surprising pleasure. You might say my senses have forever been enchanted by the stink of skunk, yet repulsed by that smell, finding it both terribly acrid and agonizingly nostalgic at the same instance. As long as it's from a distance, and the quick sniff gets quickly blown away—I do rather like it. Like someone might enjoy, in a hurting-pleasurable way, picking at a wound's dried scab.

Whenever a dog got "skunked" I did Grammom's ripe tomato trick, and in a jiff one of our rambunctious dachshunds was ready for more trouble-sniffing, out in the back woods area where I always prefer to live, if I'm not by a seashore, or atop the water on a vessel of some sort, a *stinkpot* (sailor-speak for motorboats) or, preferably a graceful-as-a-swan sailboat.

The attraction-repulsion ratio concerning skunks is shared by others besides myself. A rare person might adopt a young skunk that's been orphaned, have its scent organs (two glands on either side of its anus) surgically removed, before inviting it to live in their house. In our extended family, one such animal lover raised a skunk as a pet alongside her coterie of cats, and I'm told the skunk came to think of itself as a spoiled feline, not a member of its harsh smelling species.

Most predators, even the dangerous when wide-awake grizzly, won't touch a skunk, knowing from experience that this diminutive animal's stench hampers the best of a bear's forest reign, the skunk's clinging odor lingering long after any meager meal it might offer a hungry beast. The great horned owl is the most notorious of skunk predators, striking and killing so fast with its razor-sharp beak, severing the annoyance's thick furry neck, making any rear-end spray defense, moot.

Most animals stay far from a skunk. When threatened, before being forced to use its defensive spray, a skunk will stamp its feet, make gnashing sounds with its teeth, and do anything it can to frighten off its attackers before finally letting loose its repugnant anal blast, which can accurately hit anything it rear-aims at, up to ten feet away. Nonetheless, a skunk intuits somehow, that it takes weeks to replenish its spray, once deployed, and doesn't use this line of defense lightly—unless forced to show its superiority over an undeterred aggressor.

Like the omnivorous skunk, whose favorite food of all is honeycomb, I and perhaps you, too, need to cultivate more of this animal's defense mechanisms. We don't have to go as far as emitting bad odors, the ultimate in creating personal boundaries, guaranteed to ward off potentially dangerous attacks by most others. Because of the skunk's thick, black-and-white striped fur, it's not affected by multiple stings of bees or wasps. Thus, another great plus, however risky, of emulating skunk-hood: when Skunk smells a honey treat it gets to abscond with as much sweet nectar as it wants, undeterred by bombardier hive residents, their stingers incapable of penetrating to skunk skin.

Yes, a skunk is an expert boundary maker if ever there was one. Anyone not wanting to get blasted by its stench runs from its very sight. I sure wish I had been more skunk-like on this particular evening. Wish I'd been born with skunky glands from which I could have issued an odiferous warning against a certain person who'd ambushed me—in my own home of all places. Not a bandit, not a rapist—but an illogical fanatic.

Nearly a year had passed since the events surrounding Yusef and his congregation. My husband Will and I were at some friends' gathering where we met an intriguingly worldly couple who'd just moved to our community. The new pair had met while studying in Europe, and married in Paris twenty-some years earlier. I was right away drawn to the beautiful wife so I quickly decided to invite them for dinner at our home, our peaceful, bamboo xeriscaped retreat we'd created right in the middle of suburbia's mowed lawns. But when that evening arrived, I was unexpectedly exhausted from having been at Mother's sick bedside all day at the nursing home. She was struggling, slowly approaching her death at that time. I should have canceled the dinner plans I'd made; yes, I ought to have. But instead, I simply figured I'd explain to our new friends when they arrived that I was much too tired to prepare a meal and we could all go out for dinner. Dealing with a last-minute change in plans is something we're accustomed to in our circle, our pals easily adaptable, considerate, and jolly as carefree elves.

Additionally, when this two weeks-planned dinner finally did arrive—of all days!—it just happened to fall, without any of us quite realizing how—on the worse date of all for a get-to-know gathering with these new friends who happened to be both Muslims. The American-born wife had converted from her India immigrant-parents' Christianity to her foreign-born husband's family religion of Islam. What I had forgotten when the date was made, was how emotions ran so high among every American on this day, commemorating the fall of the twin towers. On this September 11th in the year 2016, I didn't yet know that both religious and secular people of Arabic or Islamic-Asian descent folks who'd emigrated to our country, felt equally as emotional as American-born folks did. The heated run-off for the upcoming presidential election going on just then, certainly contributed to the heightened tensions everyone was experiencing that particularly divisive year.

The first sign I had that things smelled a little *off*, that things weren't what they appeared to be, was at our front door. As I greeted our arriving guests, I noted the husband walking through our threshold ahead of his wife, carrying two bottles of wine, their contribution to my phantom dinner.

Hmmm, I thought to myself, *guess these folks are not observant religious. I thought alcohol is forbidden in Islam. But what do I know?*

"I'm afraid to say this," I said in as cheery a tone as I could muster after such an arduous day, "but I am simply way too done-in after tending to my poor sick mom today. I'm afraid we're going to have to go out tonight. Or call in a delivery order, instead of having that nice homemade dinner I promised to make for us. I'm sorry, I just don't have the juice to cook, even though I've been looking forward to spending more time with you two."

"That won't be necessary," the husband abruptly said with a big grin. "We're good. We don't need to go out. We'll stay here because you invited us here," he said, glancing at both Will's and my plainly astonished faces. Then the man gleefully added as he stood by the plate, "I see you have some cheese and crackers: perfect with the wine! That's all we need."

I sputtered something ridiculous with a half laugh, thinking this guy must be pulling my leg. I was hungry; Will was too, I knew. We wanted a meal, not a nibble.

I said, "Well, Will and I need something more substantial than snacks. So we'll chat a bit, have a drink, and then we'll go to this cute place we love, around the corner."

A short time afterwards, I brought up about being hungry and how we were ready to go out for dinner. Again, the husband brazenly insisted, "No, that's all right. We'd prefer to stay in tonight. We'll come back some other night to get that nice meal you *promised us.*" Was I mistaken, I wondered? Did his tone sound a bit less good natured than before, before worship of *the Grape* had begun? His wife kept silent, her eyes lowered; her smile, strained.

Several times I again tried suggesting we go out to eat before I realized this man was adamant. He just wanted to drink wine, and peck at the plate of gruyere, olives, and crackers I'd put out. Will helped pour both of the men more wine, while the wife sipped from her original glass; and teetotaler me, well, plain lemony water is my exciting beverage of choice.

Pretty soon things started to heat up.

On one side of our living room, Will was engrossed in conversation with the wife as they sat facing each other, while on the other side of our long white couch, the husband sat with his legs casually crossed speaking rapidly, to only me. After Will replenished the husband's second, then third glass, our guest's racing words morphed into what felt to me like double-, then triple-speak.

I remained silent as he repeatedly said, in broken-record fashion, "You people! Making our lives so difficult since 9/11! *You people* treat us Muslims so unfairly, so suspiciously!"

I sat silently, feeling absolutely stung by his words.

I hadn't expected this. Forced to feel so on the defensive, in my own home, at that! I tried to interrupt him, many times, tried to calm the man's nonstop rant. But, I couldn't. After my futile, pleasantly-given entreaties, I finally raised my voice.

"Please! I am *not* 'you people'," I said. "I am *me*, a new person to you. Someone you barely know."

My anxious voice caused the wife to glance over at us. I could tell Will was determined to keep her and himself out of the erupting fracas he saw was clearly happening, just a few yards away. I quickly noted the woman and my life partner were acting dumb, helpless, or unwilling to rescue me.

The husband did not miss a beat. It was as if he was anticipating a full-blown argument. Sitting rigidly upright now, he was on the very edge of his seat, fully engaged for battle, evidently loving to disagree with me. I was stunned. I'm not a debater. I walk away from aggression, confrontation, and blowhards of all kinds. But, I couldn't here: it was my own home, after all. Will and the wife were so engrossed (or pretending to be) in their own conversation, they did a great job of ignoring their spouses: one jovially sparring; the other, sadly being forced into it.

Both of them hear us. They just don't want any part of what I'm stuck with. Come on, save me! I silently implored Will.

I felt trapped. Plus I was utterly exhausted. And now *this*? Where oh where were my skunk-like formidable qualities *now*? The husband seemed to ramp it up even more, sensing my hesitation, my weakness.

"You *Americans* treat us Muslims all the same, like we're terrorists! Like we're personally to blame for 9/11," he roared at the top of his lungs.

Again, I shot a look of knotted-brow desperation over at my absent protector. Still, nothing. *I'm going to get Will later, for abandoning me,* I cursed my beloved, completely forgetting everything about ever having wanted to be a hybrid vigor, much less even remember what that was, right then.

Realizing I was alone, I looked at my adversary, took a deep breath and spoke firmly, "Wait! You're doing the same thing you claim we Americans do to you: you're unfairly accusing me! And besides, you're one of us now. Didn't you just tell me you've recently become a bona-fide naturalized citizen?"

This tripped up the man's momentum—for two breaths at least, another sip of wine's worth.

Now things were really smelly, and far, far from serene in my beautiful home sanctuary.

Sober as a judge, I was crawling out of my skin. All I wanted was to get away from this pushy man and get some real food. Tired and upset—feeling so helpless having earlier been painfully subjected to Mom's deteriorating condition—I was more fragile than I knew, having used up, way beyond my usual capacity, my strong resistance to life's many woes. Will and the wife remained engrossed, happily in denial. I envied my man talking to the nicer of the two folks sitting in our home. Right then I should have stood up, stamped my feet, swung my body back and forth sidewise, and ground my gnashing teeth, like a threatened badass skunk would do. But I was too wimpy, and did nothing—so I tried words again.

"Calm down, please," I begged the man, trying the nice voice on again. "Can't you just relax, and have a good time? I'm sorry that this happens to be the anniversary of that terrible day. If any of us had had the foresight to remember, I'm sure none of us would have wanted to meet tonight."

I must have punched his wound with those feeble words of mine.

"You people won't let us live in peace!" he yelled, "no matter what we do."

Okay, I have to admit it. Here, I did the most non-HV thing a person could ever do. I resorted to my reptilian, unconscious self. I miserably failed my espoused calling, letting down my fellow evolved beings. I failed my own Self, too. I let my lowly stinking-self sink into the primordial mud of no-consciousness other than—survival …

—and completely lost it!

I couldn't take it anymore! I jumped out of my chair with both my hands clamped to my ears, shouting as loudly as I could while scrambling in panic out of the room, "STOP! You have to *stop*! Stop yelling that it's all our fault!"

It's true—even the best of us HVs, wannabes, Higher-Ups or lieutenants, as I am, in the Army of Love—we all lose it sometimes.

My eyes burst with hot spears of tears as I ran to the bathroom and locked the door, sobbing, adrenalin-pummeled, terrified as if being pounced on by a zombie Halloween nightmare.

I fully broke down in my own guest bathroom. If a stranger had seen me, they'd have to think I'd just escaped being decapitated by a murderous madman chasing me. My chest heaving like a dying fish, I leaned on the bathroom sink for support, blinded by hot tears.

"teZa?" the meek voice of the wife came through the wooden door a few minutes later. "Are you all right?"

"No, I'm not," I barely managed to squeak out between choking sobs. "Give me a minute. I'll be out soon."

Later, after they left, Will told me with his mischievous grin, "Thank God you lost it, babe."

I wanted to chastise him for not rescuing me, but then he full-face grinned at me as if he figured I'd planned it, had lost my cool on purpose, like some sick Dick Chappelle freaky stage-skit or something, just to gross everybody out. Like losing my dignity, my spiritual center, was part of the setup of this slick act of mine.

"I made an ass of myself!" I wailed to this person I call my soul-match, whose sense of fairness, of rightness I've always felt attuned to, whose way of living helped me feel safe and sometimes even, understood.

"Because," he said with a vigorous nod, "that clearly was the only way we'd ever get that egomaniac to shut the fuck up!"

Will shook his head, almost laughing but not quite. But then, why not, why shouldn't my heart-mate, my illuminated, always-fun man, help me make light of something so awful? I relaxed. We marveled together, amazed about how ridiculously surreal it had been. A war erupting right in the middle of our peaceful temple. How quickly it began, went overboard, and how we felt immediately at peace, as soon as they'd left. Relieved they'd left so quickly. Will and I remarked how this reminded us of choices we get to make every moment of every day. Grateful for our resilience of Oneness, we two lovers.

Enjoying this mate of mine who always sees the sublime paradox in life, the bright side of everything, just when I need him to, I smiled at him, my drum's steady beat. Will, who always reminds me to see the irony, the need to shine laughter and love upon life's messiest muck. To let life unfold naturally, so remembrance, resolution and finally, peaceful acceptance can be restored, balancing out, calming once again, the muddy, disturbed waters of this journey of life we're on together.

My great comforter. The love of my life, Will.

Most people can agree on this much: feeling safe and thriving together on earth—these things are more important than needing to be right.

In a dream ... I hover above the sea.

Below, lying motionless on a clear patch of the white sandy bottom, I spy a kite-shaped darkness. I know immediately it's a giant ray, either a stingray or a manta. Species now vulnerable to endangerment, their possible extinction threatened in the near future. I've seen manta rays performing their enigmatic style of thrusting themselves high above the water's surface while I've been underway on quietly wind-humming, motor-less sailboats. I've been mesmerized by watching them toss themselves wildly, peculiarly up in the air, sometimes fifteen or more feet high, doing straight up belly-flops, or in spectacular somersaults and back-flips—for reasons still considered debatable by scientists.

Some speculate that the odd habit of large rays jumping high in the air off coastal shores is to shake off parasites, or to compete in mating rituals, while others proclaim the exuberant displays serve to quickly reverse the animals' direction as they're sieving organisms through their wide, open-mouthed filters as they plow the waters in the opposing direction of a fast-moving stream of micro-critters, such as krill or plankton. I first witnessed this impressive manta-show as I approached the Pacific coastline of the Panama Canal, on our sailboat's way to the Caribbean Sea. I instantly recognize the ray's underwater horned-shape silhouette in my dream.

Back to dreaming me ... as natural as another sea creature, I tread water right above the triangular shaped, completely still form that lies several fathoms below me. The animal must sense me, perhaps also intuiting as I am, that I am supposed to be with her. Yes, I dream-know it's a female. I have no gear on, no mask, and my challenged lungs aren't capable of much more than an exploratory short dive to check on her.

Suddenly, her form floats up to me. Here she is the very next instant, right before me. Looking deeply into my eyes, the ray and I know we are family. Her face is what I can only describe as a wet she-wolf, but with smooth seal-type skin, not fur; completely bizarre, I know, but such are the weird symbolisms of dreams. I am only the scribe here, remember, not an interpreter. She morphs. In one flash she's a smooth headed stingray shape, the next, a larger manta ray with distinct "devil horns" some call them.

We make deep contact. Our souls merge through our linked eyes. Our hearts. Our minds. We know each other, without gesture or sound uttered between us. With upturned watery ears, hers are big black wolf-eyes, her face has remarkably sympathetic canine features. Then, the she-wolf sting-manta ray breaks our gaze just as suddenly as she had drilled hers into mine. With no hesitation she ducks her head and rushes the short distance into my side. She burrows her head between my strong body and my treading-water, outstretched undulating arms. I immediately know the ray, her entire species, needs my solid comfort.

She nestles her fluid-feeling wing-arms around my entire torso. I give way to any resistance. The ray becomes a part of me, and I, of her.

Together we remain, clinging as one entwined body, treading the clear warm ocean sea.

Time stops still.

Because we know.

Together, we sense her life is fading. It's been so hard. Hampered by toxic seas, confusion, desperation, deadly encroaching acts by humanity, marauding giant ship-factories plundering every ocean for fish to feed the whole wide world. We feel the ray needs one living, still-beating heart: mine. Our comfort is our acceptance of this union we are. Together, the she-wolf-ray's last burden, now is lifted. We witness together, because we are One.

Then, all tension, all obstacles vanish. The life-force called *ray* slowly oozes away, from "the I-ness" into "the We-ness" into … into the moving, breathing Oneness all around us. The ray's Being-ness begins to dissolve into the molecules of the sea surrounding us.

Her spirit begins to soar. The she-wolf's form needs "me" to let go, completely, to help her final, earthly act.

Our combined energies wait, patiently, as the ray slowly no longer needs to breathe.

Slowly she melts into the abyss of before-and-after existence: Absolute Consciousness. The ray fears no more. She has merged back into the endless well of Oneness from where all of us have come.

To where we all return, in time.

PART TWO

becoming a hybrid vigor

...connected to the Great Unknown...

CHAPTER 15

creatively conscious

O
bserving the magnificent Great Blue Heron has always made me breathlessly still, watching in awe. Whether the object of my fascination is standing at rest, on one leg with its head set against the biting winter wind, as I've often seen lone specimens do, while walking along a Florida shoreline on a blustery January day; or, in the tropics, along with thousands of its primordially squawking brethren, as it roosts in the mangroves outside my houseboat's open-louvered window when it was anchored in the magical lagoon of St. Thomas. Other times, I'd notice the bird's swooping graceful flight as it alighted on a tall tree's perch, from where it could observe everything in the area; taking off quickly if a creature of any sort, other than its mate, came too close.

The Great Blue Heron has taught me a lot. From carefully observing it, I have learned patience and perseverance; but most of all—detachment.

Sometimes the majestic creature flies in a flock. Sometimes it stands by itself for hours at end, waiting, watching, and then—striking! with quick precision at exactly the right time when a right-size fish happens by. The Great Blue's disposition is not regulated by its species, but varies individually. I feel similarly about my position in our family of blended humans.

Sometimes I'm a member of the whole, whether of my immediate family group, or as part of the interconnectedness of all in existence. Nevertheless, I align myself with being hopeful, even when the tides of others' sentiments flow against a particular stance of mine.

But at other times, maintaining a spiritual position is like a solitary heron's standing on one leg, balancing steadfastly with head upright, pointing directly into the oncoming strong wind as winter's harshness blasts full force.

It's not easy being a loner, but some creatures must.

Every human who is alive experiences consciousness. If a person breathes—even if deeply in a coma, appearing to be unconscious to those on the outside—within each of us who breathes, we experience life. We are surviving.

For an individual to know and feel "Being Alive" (I'm told by coma-surviving friends), as long as we can breathe, either on our own or through artificial means, we are conscious. Breath, even if we're not cognizant of its functioning—is the first level of aware-ness. It's the basic necessity of consciousness. Those of us who've learned to be in tune with our breath, observe it, watch it, follow it, keep it in the forefront of our awareness—we're already well on our way to becoming more conscious, we hybrid vigors.

Breath is the most important thing about being alive. That's why any person who can breathe, whether on our own or with medical aid, experiences the base level of awareness, as it's called in the yogic chakra-study of consciousness. That's why *breathing* is equally a human's most fundamental aspect of existence, while at the same time, focusing on the *in- and out-breath* is the most profound tool for each of us to become ever more acutely, expansively aware. A person who is not aware of how important it is to be in tune with their breath has not yet expanded their percep-tions, beyond that of life's basic necessities.

After acquiring survival skills, the second level of awareness activates: this is the seat of emotional energies. Many creatures have emotional lives, not just humans. The emotional level of consciousness is where the creative *thrust of Beingness* is experienced. This second energy center, or chakra, is where urges arise from our *wanting* to do things, to make things. Here, we express, by our creating skills, our ability *to feel* things. Sadly, some individuals never admit the importance of theirs or other people's emotions. Or are unwilling to accept, and work with the idea of healing them, when their own emotional selves have been injured or undeveloped. These types of humans experience inner turmoil, perhaps their entire lifetime, especially if they continue to deny the importance of human feelings.

If one observes a very young child (or chimpanzee, or another simian) you'll see them wanting to touch with their fingers and toes every single thing around them. Pick it up, feel it, squeeze it, roll it in their hands, bite it, smell it. A parent works hard so their offspring doesn't ingest or stick small objects up a nose or down a throat. Human progeny, as an intelligent, rational thinking species, naturally want to *feel* and *explore* every single thing we can. Sometimes, of course, as parents and caretakers, we have to limit our children's explorations. "Don't touch the fire!" "Don't go near that rattlesnake!" "Stop kicking your sister!"

I was a full-custodial stepparent, sometimes even an oxy-moronic single-stepparent when Will went off on a movie set for weeks at a time, and I was then obliged to guide and direct our two young children, alone. It was my duty to point out what was good as well as not-so-good, fun as well as dangerous, helping them to figure out the go-green from the red off-limits of childhood.

Even if they're abandoned at birth, all Nature's critters teach their offspring the best way to survive. Abandonment in animals happens occasionally, but these drastic measures, fulfill the parental role of helping certain species to more successfully stay alive. This doesn't work with human children, however. Abandonment, whether emotional, spiritual, or physical, severely damages a young human psyche.

Every person experiences emotional energy on pretty much a

constant basis, unless they're in a suspended state such as in a coma. When a young person who has received proper guidance reaches adolescence, their energy in the emotional realm starts to become activated much more intensely than it had in earlier childhood. That's why hormonal teens are so emotionally barraged, needing more guidance at this crucial stage of their development.

At the same time as an adolescent's emotions rise up, sometimes in volcanic forces, so too does a person's urge to express their creativity. Both these urges originate from the same source, the next-to-survival level of awareness. Young children make and play and want to do everything. They create games out of sticks, leaves, spoons, dust bunnies, anything! Kids play with mud puddles, or … whatever's around. I ate dirt when I was a kid. I thought mud tasted pretty yummy, but really, it was my ebullience playing pretend-chef that made my tiny mud pies taste so … acceptable. I also ate rolled-up balls of paper (hmmm?) and wanted to draw, paint, build, play, try and do everything I could. I climbed trees, recklessly so, and as a result of a bad fall from one, have dealt with scoliosis since. Not a tragedy, it turns out, because my affliction prompted my *seeking-out* relief which led to a yoga practice that began in my teens, over fifty years ago. This is a case of what appears to be a "bad thing" (the tree fall) developing into a "good thing": my resulting lifelong *love* of yoga and meditation.

This need-to-know-and-feel-everything is part of the second wave, the rising-up of a shared, universal consciousness, which all humans naturally have, if recognized and nurtured properly. To be curiously creative is our human desire. It's our birthright, to make, to do, to feel, to explore. To climb to the top of every mountain we can, and descend to the depths of Earth's great trenches, as long as we have the energy and strength to do so. That's why so many of us exercise as much as we do, to maintain our energy levels, so we can keep up our explorations for as long as we can. This is also why some of us are avid readers or film buffs, because books and movies allow us to have adventures in our hyperactive minds, if we can't get enough real adventures with our physical bodies for any variety of reasons.

Like all artists, I think a lot about emotions, mine and others'. From early on, I knew *feelings* were the root of all creativity. After basic training in the visual arts, learning about various materials, colors, anatomy, perspective and spatial relationships and other elements of composition, I came to trust the impulses that arose from within me. When I make a work of art, whether written or visual, I never doubt when the inner Voice of my instincts tells me to "use blue" instead of another color; or "put a beach here" instead of a horizon or a mountain in a landscape. Or to make a 3-dimensional form (a sculpture) instead of 2-dimensions (a flat plane, like a painting or drawing).

When my emotional center dictates, "Do this, creatively"—I've learned to obey that *inner command*. From training myself, I've come to trust this creative urge I feel so strongly. I've learned that when I want to create, as all humans must, not just us artists—I have to trust my *gut feeling*, the *indicator* coming from my inner font of inspiration. (This "gut feeling" is the instinctual psychic ability of a person's third chakra, also called the "solar plexus," which is the root-cause of taking action, which happens when a person owns who they are, known as their *personal power*.)

As an example, when I'm exposed to an artist, such as when I met the masterful Hundertwasser, his work stimulated my recognizing-greatness *gut-button*, while another artist's work could register an absolute zero on my inner *interested-in-this* scale, indicating a lack of my gut response.

I came to trust this emotional response of mine, which, when activated, feels like a kicking in my navel. This center of energy I never wanted to intellectualize about. I just wanted to trust those feelings, which, after years of copying during my learning phase, allowed me to create new ideas instead of comparing or judging mine, or mimicking other original works.

I just want *to Be*, when I create. Not to discern too much, just enough to make outrageous stuff (eliminate the trite, redundant, or pedantic). Of course, this took years of training and practice. I gave this blossoming awareness of original creativity my permission to be activated. I never felt obliged to follow the latest whims, fads or fancies as they shifted, which is called by the critics, derivative art.

Like the great blue heron, I never planned to stand strong and alone, against the overpowering winds of conformity and propriety. Sometimes, sure, I felt ostracized for being too different, too spiritual, *too out-there,* too—against the norm. The creative spirit I am screams, wanting to express shocking *Wake Up!* art, my medium of preference.

That's why early in my efforts of uncovering original-ideas in my work, I became very adept at detaching, in order to continue making art without losing my soul to the seduction of commercial-ism.

One person wants to create a new way to explore space (like Elon Musk) while another is perfectly at ease, simply existing on Earth (such as a tribal indigenous living in a grass hut). The latter person is happy to, let's say, never leave his isolated village on the edge of the Sahara, but enjoys creating a trap for a wild animal that will serve as dinner for that night. Both Musk and the African bushman use their creative energies in very different ways, but similarly.

Both are using other faculties along with satisfying their urge to create.

Elon is focusing his awakened energy of consciousness (after amassing his personal fortune) toward benefiting the future of humankind; whereas the Sahara tribal fellow is happy to make a meal for himself and his family, and probably isn't even thinking about how the rest of the world is faring as he sets his trap of woven vines. Both Musk and the hunter, however, are most likely equally using their creative energies to full capacity.

My first creative thrust was initiated by feeling absolutely gaga about God, or Love. I've wanted to explore and document the Great Mystery that spontaneously arose within me, ever since I was very young. I couldn't get enough of fairy tales, magical stories, church rituals, prayers, incense, candles—anything that made me feel connected to the Great Unknown. And the stranger, more personal the contact with the Mystery, like communing with bees and other wild animals that happened to come close by me, the happier I was. Raised by one parent who was religious and the other, an agnostic, right from the start of exploring this God-thing on my own, I knew there were choices, because my parents had such different views about the Source of Being.

I never felt confused, until drugs and booze entered the picture. But that was as much a necessary step in my journey as my early initiation into meditation. Each step in my spiritual development felt exciting, as if I were getting closer to some *Big Truth* that I first felt inside me, which kept directing me to know more. I saw how different I was from my mother's strict religiosity, just as I was from my father's open-to-all-possibilities, no-answers approach to life. I knew there had to be *something else* going on other than what people said was *real*. As I explored more, I saw this questionable approach to what I called the *God-thing*, revealed in as many different ways of expression as there are different kinds of life forms.

I felt particularly close to the God-energy when I taught myself how to draw. I did this in secret because … it was *my* special way to *feel* closer to the Mystery, by creating something from nothing. Each time I drew a lifelike bird or a flower, I felt closer to the essence others sometimes call God. More inquisitive, as I neared adolescence, I began creating by copying, but always in secret, because I was forever getting in trouble and didn't want to be told "No." After animals and plants from encyclopedia photos, I began drawing female nudes from my father's hidden-away Playboy mags I'd discovered. To me, the human animal, the unclothed, unaltered male and female form, held the key to the ultimate in beauty, grace, and design, its muscled skin, fleshed-out complexities as thrilling and complex as any landscape, still-life, or dream scene.

To my art-apprentice young self, nudity was about a person being in their spirit body, without the heavy unnaturalness of that entity's true essence being covered. Nudity was never about sex stuff, when I was learning to trust what inspired me to make art.

Anything that inspires or excites us is our creative energy being stimulated. If a certain type of music or entertainment moves you, this is second-chakra energy stimulation. If you want to visit Transylvania to see the birthplace of Bram Stoker, the original Dracula—this is creative energy at work, so pay attention. If you want to play the drum and not the violin that you were urged to by your mother, your creative consciousness is the reason why you must follow your own gut feeling. Which is another way of saying *owning your own power.*

"Follow your bliss," was how Joe Campbell put it. Of course, we learn to distinguish what kinds of bliss are good for us from what aren't. We shouldn't eat a bucket of gummy bears, but maybe every child has to try, at least once, in order to see how sick too much sugar makes us. Maybe we have to drink too much booze once or twice, or a hundred times, to understand why being drunk sucks. Maybe getting sick won't be enough to stop some over-indulgers, like I used to be. As sexual beings, we don't necessarily *have* to hook up with every single person who turns us on ... because ... that'll give us an STD and a rotten reputation, not to mention complex dramas to deal with. The list goes on and on about how each of us gets to learn, by discovering how to use awareness signals we have emanating from our awakened energy centers.

The other, just as important urge—part of this second (out of the seven chakras) level, the creative level of human consciousness—is human sexuality. One of the great marvels of Nature: Sex!

I for one couldn't miss what the sexual urge was all about, because early in life I was hit on top of the head with others' sexual urges.

At age ten I was sexually taken advantage of, *toyed with* by a drunk uncle.

And then—shortly afterwards—I happened to witness a naked man "doing something weird with his hands *down there*," as he stared straight at me from where he sat trying to hide on steps that went below ground level. He was in a place where he shouldn't have been and where I happened to be, innocently and *accidentally*. It would be decades later, when I'd find out this aberration I'd witnessed was my naked, Illinois small town's elderly parish priest, masturbating while perversely staring at me behind his creepy dark sunglasses, ludicrously trying to hide under a wide-brimmed yellow straw hat. I alighted from the bicycle I was riding alone, around the circular sidewalk of my closed-for-the-summer grade school, where this isolated event took place, across the wide-open field from where my house was. The pathetic old priest had hidden himself in the shadows of the empty school's dark subterranean staircase that led to below-ground classrooms.

If having been abused by a family member, on top of the awfulness of seeing this ugly priest-scene (it was my mother who told me, in my thirties), both horrendous abuses of my childhood's innocence by controlling-adults, if these weren't enough already to warrant a lifetime of neurosis about Sex for me to deal with—the biggest hurdle of all was yet to come.

The first young man whom I fell madly in love with, who I thought was surely my very own Prince Charming ... turned out to prefer other men. I only found that out after years of our being together in blissful union, well, nearly, except for the sex part, which wasn't a problem until the end. We were both Nature freaks, you see. He, a botanist, and I, his illustrator. When Tim died so sadly, at age forty-four, seventeen years after we broke up, he was one of the earliest victims of the HIV pandemic. It broke my spirit, losing him. Romantically first, then again when he actually died. He was my match in so many ways. But no matter: he preferred Sexing his own gender. I was mortified when he died so tragically, wasted and prematurely. And, even though it'd been so long since we'd separated, grief threw me into a disorienting spiral that took me by complete surprise. Still, I was relieved I didn't test positive when I nervously went for my AIDS test.

Perhaps, you'll now see why it was personally so important for me to comprehend the *hugeness* of the sexual urge, so compellingly strong in so many of us. For me, when it came to understanding the Power of Sex, I first had to understand the Power of Spirit. In order to understand why my botanist, as much as we loved each other, had to follow his own Truth, without me as his soul-match. To do this, I had to embrace my own Truth. It took years, but when I finally understood, when I accepted that Tim had to fulfill his own destiny as a gay man, that's when my heart and soul truly began to heal. This only happened after I became a sober woman, found my teacher, and ... traded my addiction to self-loathing for my new addiction ... of Self Love, the God-thing within.

Hopefully, by sharing my story, people will be able to better understand these dual inner forces do arise from the same energy center. A mysterious connection that eluded me for far too long.

I am sure of only one thing: God is Love. And Love is where I put my energies above all other things. I'm a person who happens to have been born female, and that's okay with me. I've got bigger and better things to think about, and do, than to think about other people's gender issues. I've had a hard-enough time sorting out my own, thank you very much. Being an incested child ain't easy in the sex-identity category, let me assure you. After getting sober, I learned to accept that both Sex and Spirit are huge energies for all us humans to contend with: both fascinatingly wonderful, and problematically weird, at the same time. After losing my botanist, I made sure I was free to explore my sexuality all I needed or wanted. I was driven, you see, to escape anyone ever controlling or hurting me again. Today, thanks to my spiritual soulmate, my consort Will, exploring my sexuality no longer has a consuming pull on me as it once did, back when I was attempting to figure out how to dance with its strong inner force.

Why my Prince of long-ago preferred men; that was a life-altering conundrum for me. It took me years before I found peace, and forgave him, forgave myself too, for loving so deeply my bi-botanist, who chose to go gay, after me. Ultimately, he sacrificed his life for that choice. I can accept that today. Do I still have mixed feelings about his choice? Like I've said, I focus on positives. I don't allow my mind to go down that rabbit hole anymore. I respect Tim's choice, although I can't say I understand it.

Losing my fairy tale Prince to other men was the reason, the last push, for my having once given up hope. That heartbreak pushed me over the edge, head-first, into the dangerous-rapids, tumultuous life of a full-blown addict who had given up caring what happened to her. Trying to forget what I couldn't accept, was my drug of choice. Today, I am different, I am sober. I have learned to accept Tim's choice. Did it take a lot of work, self-enquiry type of work? Yes. Lots. But I wanted to, and chose to live in the Light, not the darkness of rejection, despair, or misunderstanding anymore.

I truly believe we can't understand all that's involved in life. *Things are not what they appear to be.* Some things, we just have to accept. Or else, by not accepting *what is,* we continue to choose a life of unhappy misery.

Being happily married to Will, my equal partner in all respects, is my reward for having been patient and kind with myself, not judging or denying who and what I am, and who my botanist was. I am a person who chose to explore sexuality as fiercely, as creatively, as I now cultivate my spirituality. Some of us manage to explore both realms of our creative energies, sexual and spiritual at the same time, while others never get to fully experience either realm. I am fortunate to have been born with the desire to explore the myriad aspects of my humanness: my emotional-mental feelings; my physicality, my sexual and psychic animalness; and my spiritual-ity—all aspects of each of ours beingness.

I happened to be talking once to an obstetrician who had delivered many babies in his decades-long practice. "It's a well-known fact," the seasoned doctor said, "that there is a minimum of three sexes. Every doctor who deals with large numbers of newborns knows there are males, females, and an indeterminate, in-between sex, in which the baby's genitalia can vary from having both a vagina and a penis, to having remnants of either. Every gender variable in a human can happen, just as it happens to plants and other animals. When it comes to the physical characteristics of a newborn's sexuality, I've seen every possible combination. Every baby is different. Every person has the right to discover their own way of being, with the sexual equipment they've been born with."

Sex is a mystery, that's all there is to it. A big Mystery right up there with Spirit (God), and Life (Existence) itself.

If someone else wants to make Sex more important than Spirit, that's their choice. For me, after having explored my sexuality with almost obsessive abandon, today I'm happy to focus on exploring my spiritual connection to existence. Having a solid and fulfilling relationship with Will for almost three decades now, allows me to do so. Why would I want to change what turns me on the most? I'm addicted to the Mystery of Mysteries. The Nameless Spirit that guides my life and All that is. Fortunately, I chose a mate who feels similarly and has a similar past. Today, our explorations are shared: spiritual, intellectual, and, best of all, fun and sexy beyond measure.

If it wasn't enough being forced to sort out my screwed-up feelings that resulted from having been sexually toyed with (I hate the word *abused*) as a child, then, after losing my man-loving Prince, that's when life kidnapped me on a detour into addiction. I dove into the very dark, very low place of Self-forgetting. Now, in retrospect, I see how I needed to experience this shock, of losing that man's love over the ridiculous reason of his and my happenstance gender preference. Like a cosmic joke, my heartbreak forced me to seek out Spirit, so I could heal. I had to have a *sex shock* that took me so far down, literally, to hating my Self, the lowest I've ever been, in order to be able, in an equal yet opposite measure, to fly as high in discovering, and understanding the salvation of Self Love, when I learned to heal my brokenness.

It's good to openly talk about how the power of Sex can push some of us into seeking Spirit, as part of our healing from whatever hurt us. Ostracized, standing strong against the wind of a few others' opinion, I stand strong and sure, like the Great Blue Heron against the winter wind. Labeled a "social media whore" by some family members who misunderstand my motives about so freely sharing about healing from life's early traumas, I stand stalwart, alone if I must.

In today's world, we need to discuss the elephants in the living room, not cover them up or pretend they don't exist. For far too long, deviant sex (along with H's pet projects of recycling our shit and our bodies, disposing of both in a more *natural* manner) has been an uncouth subject in "polite society." The #MeToo awareness has made the topic of intrusive sex finally acceptable, and necessary, and I, along with multitudes of others, are appreciative of this liberating honesty. The sexual energy is too strong a force to leave un-discussed, especially when people—men or women, in-betweens, boys or girls—cross boundaries and invade other people's sacred space, whether physically or emotionally.

Remember—the two are closely related.

The twin energies—of sexual (of the material realm), and spiritual (non-material)—which of these two energies will eventually take precedence in our individual experiences? The answer has to do with Nature versus nurture, mentoring, and personal goals we all get to choose for ourselves.

Both expressions, Sex and Spirit, are of a person's own creative force, completely aligned with one's personal will in healthy, well-balanced individuals. But if either expression of a person's Beingness is not given enough nurturing in the adolescent stage of life, or is desecrated by another's debased morality (in the case of sexual or emotional abuse of any kind), or by accidental circumstances, that young person's sexual or spiritual nature can be seriously harmed or hampered. For anyone whose sexual energy field was damaged by a controlling, outside force or influence, such as mine was—whether by a controlling person (a horny priest, a drunken relative) or a cultural aberration (I venture to say that Western society gives sex an obsessive importance in today's celebrity-deified culture)—I'm happy to report that cultivating one's spiritual energy is the antidote that will heal any damage to a person's inner Self.

So closely aligned are they, that the light of Spirit has the ability to *heal the harm* done by the dark uses of Sex. Balanced individuals enjoy developing both their sexuality and spirituality, along with the emotional and physical facets of their healthy natures. Such people delight in the ability to experience comfort and complete satisfaction with spiritualized sex.

These two energies, Spirit and Sex, are twin-like in their mutual ability to exert either positive or negative influences, healthy or toxic, over an individual's entire life experience. So closely aligned are these second-chakra forces, in fact, that this is evidenced by the human urge to PRO-create, the natural way for all species to CREATE. Whether making a cake (a *creative drive*), or a child (the animalistic, original function of *sexual drive*), both these energies in humans are intertwined. This is why we hear so often in the news about the abuse of power by respected spiritual leaders, who ultimately fail their calling by confusing their highly developed spiritual energies with their unfortunately, un-spiritualized sexual urges.

Confusion results about *what actually is* the spiritual side of our nature. In some people's lives, spiritual includes the enjoyment of our pleasurable sexual-side as well, for sex is not just about baby-making procreation, we all know that. When the sexual side of our nature has been overly cultivated though, or exclusively promoted to the exclusion of its twin, the spiritual yearning goes dormant within our inner Self, awaiting a time when our innate desire to know *It* will arise—and our yearning to know Spirit will again manifest in our everyday life.

When ... the time is right.

One twin is named, *sexual drive*, the other is called, *spiritual yearning*. The two energies originally, naturally arise, practically simultaneously in an individual's life, right after we've learned, hopefully, our survival skills from whatever caretakers we have. First, we learned to seek shelter, clothe our chilly bones, and feed our hungry stomachs. After that, we get creative in seeking our life's fulfillment. Happening at the same time as the awakening of our sexuality, at the very onset of puberty, is the arising of our spiritual energy. Our sexuality, therefore, is just as important a part of our quest to know our true, whole selves, as embracing our spiritual nature allows us, and vice versa.

If Sex and Spirit *urges* are not cultivated and guided properly, they either get too much or too little attention. In modern times, the energy of Sex predominates over that of Spirit, because of cultural pressure and conditioning. With no nurturing attention given it, a young person's spiritual yearning goes back to a state of dormancy, within the inner Self. When this happens, an individual's sexuality usually becomes the most predominant side of our nature, subject to the norms of the materialistic culture in which we live. For most Westerners, that means plenty of sex and not much spirit. If a certain person is fortunate, and their spiritual nature is nurtured by healthy guidance upon its awakening, no matter at what stage of life, it's each person's individual responsibility to keep this spiritual energy *alive* within us. Practices such as choosing good company, fostering good thoughts, and choosing right action are helpful, but especially difficult things for the wild-and-crazy, hormone-riddled younger years, when, let's face it, having sex is way more fun than meditating alone, say.

Since today's mainstream culture accentuates sex (lusty sells more products!), leaving spirit out in the cold, un-talked about, unacknowledged, disregarded entirely in many instances, it's no wonder that teens virtually forget about their dormant urge, their spirituality. Think back to those teenage years; do you remember? Do you recall asking yourself:

"I wonder who I am?

"I wonder what I'm here for?

"I wonder where I'm going after death?"

I certainly remember, vividly. When adolescence rolled in, I was reeling from the explosion in my private world that resulted from having been sexually exploited. I'd been exposed to more than my share of other's misbehaving debauchery. That, unfortunately, resulted in my entire teens being plagued by repeated nightmares, from which I'd awaken in cringing, shivering terror, the pillow wet from my tears.

In the day, I'd be freaked about each night's sleep always ending in being pursued and tortured. At one point, at eighteen, I was convinced I was insane. Going to sleep became extremely anxiety-producing for me. And when I did fall asleep, for years afterwards, I'd awaken several times throughout the night with the same repeat-nightmare of what had actually happened, dream-warped and weepy-weird distorted. The transgressions I'd suffered got replayed every night, damn! Going to sleep became my personal dread that never ended. Until—out of desperation, by this time in college, skipping classes so I could take short take naps instead of experiencing the nightly sex-horror show—I finally agreed to take some acid. Which miraculously ended the stuck-ness my self-flagellating mental loop had been stuck in since the abuse occurred.

That's why I can reaffirm that the current use of *micro-doses* of LSD and other psychotropics do indeed work, to relieve a sufferer's repeated, endlessly, psychological torment. Being stuck in negative loops of the brain's self-destructive thinking can be stopped. But, as I'd later find out, learning to meditate, using a mantra to still my obsessive-compulsive, overactive mind, works best of all. Yes, meditation takes discipline, which a lot of people balk at. But the relief is permanent and thoroughly risk-free.

Whether you're a bona fide homo sapiens or a true blue hybrid vigor, calling yourself this Self-proclaimed state, simply *when you're ready*—everyone has a spiritual life (whether it's been awakened or not), plus a libido (however high or low), a physical body (fit or not), and emotional side (off- or well-balanced) as well. We are intended to discover and enjoy all parts of ourselves, to the best of our abilities, and explore any opportunity to become a wholly healed, and happy person.

Propagation of our species is a biological necessity. So naturally, the sexual energy is a big deal, strongly present for the vast majority of everyone alive. Very few of us are asexual beings. That's why desiring to mate, to *have progeny* (or its funky cousin, just plain wanting to *hook up*) comes right after our species' innately learning to survive. It took me longer than most of my peers to figure out this simple fact, because my sense of "self" had been crushed from the sexual improprieties of others. My life's challenges compelled me to discover answers to get un-crushed, which a lot more people need to ask of themselves.

The spiritual energy of *wondering, of asking spiritual questions* will go dormant again, as it did with me, if that energy isn't nurtured upon its adolescent rising-up. It will lie asleep within us again, waiting until its awakened the next time. Spiritual yearning (the arising of the *kundalini energy*, the yogic-scriptural term) gets activated at key times throughout a person's life, if it isn't nurtured early and isn't encouraged to stay active. Usually an adulthood spiritual awakening occurs after a big shock, like someone close to us dying or some other personal tragedy. Then, the spiritual yearning will again arise in a person's awareness ... and consciousness naturally, beautifully, expands ... our natural state of Presence. A great word for expanded consciousness.

Ordinary s-e-x is an action noun-verb; it's a short-term act. Sex becomes spiritualized when people engaging in it honor the act as sacred, however that may be for them. Desiring to know what a spiritualized sexual connection *can be* is motive enough for a fully expressive creative existence, enough to inspire a person's lifetime commitment to a single partner. Like fostering a spiritual life itself, this type of sexual relationship takes stamina, flexibility, acceptance, and creative ingenuity, which certainly doesn't appeal to everyone.

Having a spiritual love match was something I'd always dreamed of, swore to never give up trying to find, and only after having given up ever being lucky enough to find it, finally found—Will.

CHAPTER 16

healing using energy

Everyone who hears our symbolic, metaphysical bird smiles at the first burst from Roostie's full throttle plea for attention. Whether deep in a dream, asleep, awake or just rousing, Roostie's prideful trumpeting helps align the proper order of the day for those of us who hear his call.

When day breaks, he announces wakefulness. When evening falls, Roostie crows to remind his hens to come back to the roost. He's summoning all who hear to take stock, count our blessings, settle in, and finally, to rest.

Whether awakening, or time for regeneration, Roostie beckons, reminds, and helps maintain the order of an otherwise chaotic, confusing world.

Roosters and hens have foxes, snakes and raccoons to watch out for.

We humans have each other more than any other type of danger, to be wary of.

Soon after I'd determined to stop pouring substances into my body, I found myself at a months' long healing workshop. During each of the seven weekly gatherings, our group would explore a different *chakra*. I'd signed up, not even knowing what a chakra was, exactly. All I knew was, I was ready to be healed from my fractured psyche, damaged in childhood from an adult's selfish actions.

When the second chakra workshop began, the attendees were split into four healing-teams comprised of three each. Taking turns, one person in each team was chosen to be "worked on" while the two others would be "the healers." Our team chose me as the first person they would work on. I was asked to lie down on the comfortable thick carpet, while the healers kneeled, one at my head, the other at my feet. The two women at either end of my body would be doing *the work* while I was instructed to relax my body, and concentrate on the chakra of that day's group attention.

The "work" entailed all three of us mentally concentrating our spiritual energies directly toward that area of the second chakra of whichever person was being worked on. This is the area below the navel and above the groin, deep within the inner body.

The neutral colored, sparse room was quiet after everyone settled into their roles. Everyone was focused on doing the work. Each of us on our team was mentally sending our personal spiritual power toward the second energy center of ... me.

Only a few minutes of silence had passed when suddenly the woman who was gently holding my head as I laid on the soft carpet, whispered loudly, "Oh my God! Do you see that!?" While at the same moment the woman who was holding my feet exclaimed as quietly as she could, "Shit yes! What the hell *is that*?!"

I popped my head up. "What? What is it?" I asked, not as quietly. "What's going on?"

All heads in the room turned toward us.

Both healers at my head and feet, remained stunned for a moment, looking at something that I tried, but couldn't see. My neck strained upward, my eyes peered all over, but nothing was there! I plopped back down as the two women gasped and made muffled noises of alarm back and forth, trying their best not to disturb the rest of the again quiet room. Nobody else there but these two, apparently, had seen anything. The other women on my team now spoke quietly while continuing to hold onto both ends of my prone body.

"I just saw a gigantic orange ball of light," one woman whispered, "with a big black hole in it, rise up out of your second chakra!"

"I saw the exact same thing!" the other woman said. "It was a flaming ball of orange light, except for that big hole in its middle."

"Then it went *whoooosh*—and disappeared up, away from you and out of sight! Gone! In just an instant," one said.

"That's exactly what I saw, too," the other exclaimed.

"What on earth could that be?" they both asked using their own words. I remained prostate, knowing.

"I know exactly what that is," I said, instantly relieved to say it aloud. "Orange is the color of the second chakra, right?"

Both women agreed.

"Well it makes sense. I've been hurt in that area, sexually hurt. That's where spiritual and sexual energies reside, and that's where my life needs the most healing. I've been carrying around so much pain about sex, since I was ten. I always felt I was to blame for all the bad stuff that ever happened to me. Since I can remember, it's always felt like life itself is a death sentence I've been condemned to. Up until a few weeks ago, when I quit getting high, I always thought I'd be unhappy forever. That's when I decided to start forgiving myself, when I got sober. I want to heal what's damaged about me. That fucking black *thing* inside the orange ball you saw leave me? That's how I've been feeling—like my life has had a big hole inside it. I've been carrying around brokenness. But now I already feel so much better—different. Lighter. Freer."

Before we began that day, the workshop members had learned that the color associated with the second chakra is *orange*. Our leader talked about the different levels of consciousness that each of the seven chakras represent. The natural rising-up of human awareness we all can experience happens at our own pace. Before this healing, I'd not allowed myself the liberty of owning my feelings, they were too painful. It'd never been easy for me—to feel.

Getting off mood-altering substances allows feelings to surface, that's for sure.

Most people rely upon how they *feel* to judge things. Unless the history of art or literature is studied, it's hard for a lot of people to know any more than to feel, "I like that picture," or "That book didn't do it for me."

Most of us learn to trust our *feelings* that arise from within. This is emotional awareness that helps us through life's many challenges and choices. As a person grows and matures, we learn to trust our feelings, even when our feelings might go against what's expected of us.

Right after the second level of consciousness arises, comes the third level, the seat of one's personal power. Each of us gets the opportunity to embrace—or deny—our destiny, our life's purpose. When we are able to recognize our own life's purpose, we can then also, automatically, recognize other's spiritual power as well. This third level of awareness is where many of us get to experience our life's real challenge. Here, we start to ask ourself, *How do we know what is our life's purpose?* Feeling *empowered* is a great asset on the spiritual path. When we embrace our own power that's when we're *in the flow.* We let our desires to create empower us, leading us on the ever-upward spiral of one discovery after the next. Right now, the most important discoveries of all, concern our species' ability to survive, as we face these challenging toxic times in our world's environment.

When a person fully accepts responsibility for their own survival, they have reached physical maturity. This is also when their consciousness has arisen to the second, then the third level, where we accept our own personal power as unique, and truly our own responsibility.

Unless a person is on the wide spectrum of mental illness, and is cared-for by others, accepting one's own power is essential to thrive. To any challenged person, mentally, physically, or emotion-ally—we hybrid vigors compassionately send our love, and help them as best we can to function in the world. There is always room for everyone to fit into a spiritualized, more humanized society. There's plenty of opportunities for all of us to practice magnanimity, however we can, instead of selfish denial or judgment. When we come from a state of Love, there are no limits to possibilities.

Many people approaching this level of awareness, the third, where our personal will becomes aligned with the will of our Divine Nature, are simply not ready or not willing to advance. People often get ambushed by their feelings of unworthiness here, hiding behind disbelief, another mask of fear. If a person hasn't properly nurtured him-, her-, or themself, or been given enough youthful guidance by parents or caretakers, some of us have harder times learning to trust that our feelings are what they are … signals of consciousness … and we end up spending forever locked in a labyrinth of repeating, endlessly, the foibles of our youthful folly, stuck in emotional traps, trying needlessly to figure things out. That's how I happened to stay in active addiction—because the task of developing spiritual awareness was too formidable, to know, and learn to love, my inner Self.

I reported back to my workshop friends in the weeks and months after that afternoon's amazing release of the damaged orange ball of energy arising from my damaged Self. The phenomenon that the two women witnessed, visual proof of the trauma I'd sustained in childhood, released me from the self-imagined curse I had been suffering from, feeling cursed, before that day. The "black hole" aptly depicted the unhealed pain that had been trapped in my psyche since childhood, but now was released from that inner, psychological prison of mine.

No longer did my existence feel condemned or disadvantaged in any way from another person's having harmed me. From then on,

I felt like what had happened, happened. That's it. I learned to accept *What is,* and in this case, *What was.* Seems absurdly simple, but that's what happened. In time, I began to realize more insights. How the abuse I'd suffered, instead of ruining my life, had actually pushed me, forced me to explore being a spiritual seeker, probably more than if I hadn't been so damaged early in life.

Friend, know that healing can take place any time a person sets their mind to wanting to be whole again, as we all are at birth.

If you feel that you have suffered any kind of hardship or unjust treatment, remember this. Set aside some time to devote to sending some of your own spiritual energy (called *intention*) to that part of your Self you feel is injured, harmed, or not in balance. You don't have to be specific about what might have caused your feeling out-of-balance, or know which chakra or energy level got damaged. It's not even important to know what a chakra is. What *is important* is to know that you have incredible spiritual energy within your Self, your better, higher Self, that's available for you to use anytime. Start by focusing on healing your own life, your damaged smaller self. Learn to direct this invisible energy, with your intention alone, to any part of your life that you think needs mending. Go within, and give yourself a spiritual tune-up whenever you feel the need.

Simply get quiet, let your mind still (it's best done by following the breath) and then … ask your Self what you can do to help make yourself feel more whole. You will receive an answer, maybe not right away. But you will sense guidance if your consciousness is open to receiving it. Then be sure to follow the directions you receive. After some time, after you feel more whole, you can try the same exercise by asking your Higher Self: What is my Life Purpose?

Then be sure to wait for the answer. It may take days, weeks, even months. But it will come. When you receive the answer, test it if you wish. Your true life's purpose cannot be convinced to remain silent. You will know, you will recognize your Truth. Don't try denying it.

Here another suggestion in which to tune into what you need for spiritual growth.

Recall an event, past or present that causes you discomfort. Locate the place in your body in which you feel disturbed. Be specific: your gut, your head, your heart, where do you *feel* out of sorts? The key to re-birthing your Self, your Higher Self, as a hybrid vigor, is to know that you can heal your own Self. Just choose to be more whole and happier, and the healing has begun. If you want to enjoy life more than you have been, wholeness is yours for the asking. That's all it takes to be a hybrid vigor.

All things are possible when we focus on our inner spiritual power. This awe-inspiring force called Love is at our beck and command.

CHAPTER 17

#UsToo

Roostie is working double time today. Off in the distance, somewhere in a treetop, his call can be heard now in the middle of the day. I wonder what he's clamoring about this time? Maybe it's the latest news; maybe another abuser, sadly resembling a human-pig, got ratted out!

Some claim that pigs are smarter than rats. Folks who raise pigs often bring them into their family home as domesticated pets, alongside of, or instead of dogs and cats. In some European countries, feral species of hogs are raised to be killed by paying customers, and released to be tracked down on farmlands, on extravagantly expensive, organized hunts. While in more remote regions, domesticated wild boars, tightly leashed to their owners, roam dense forests digging for truffles and other fungus and roots. In dry scrubby parts of the southeastern United States, hog flesh is considered better than cow or sheep by some country folk. Neither a hunter nor truffle eater myself, my experience with Pig lies closer to my heart.

It was part of the sixties' revolutionary vernacular for us anti-Vietnam War demonstrators to call the police, *pigs*. But I always used pig as a tongue-in-cheek affectionate term because my own life was saved once by a cop who stopped me for going too slow, of all things, spaced out as I was (having ingested something mind-altering) and driving on that lonely tree-lined, Vermont hilly road. His kind-spoken warning propelled me to seek much needed help.

At that moment I had been in the middle of one of my many pre-hybrid vigor emotional *bottoms*, one of the last of the numerous mental breakdowns I'd had, before I willingly gave up trying to self-medicate my troubles away with various pills, powders and potions.

During summer visits to my grandparents' New Jersey farm, I had many chores, my favorite being the daily feeding, tending, and watching over of the pig pen. Visiting the pungently muddy enclosure as much as I could, watching the large boisterous animals interact, intrigued me no end. Even though I knew they'd soon be transformed into chops, salted hams, slices of bacon, pork stews made from the entrails, the richest part of any animal. Even the lips and ears of my beloved friends—I was well aware and accepted, as a farm girl does—would be churned into sausages, the spicy mixture my grandmother stuffed with a hand-grinder into the pigs' own emptied and cleaned-out intestines; whose half-digested contents were the only parts, besides the eyes and teeth, that weren't eaten by us hardworking farmers. Practically everything eaten on my grandparents' farm was grown there. The only edibles that weren't made at the farm were the occasional sugary treats of fresh donuts, or a loaf of squishy white sandwich bread, sliced thin, the latest invention of the fifties in America, both items delivered to Grammom's door by the festive bread truck each week.

As my Grammom said in her halting English, "Pig is pig. Cow is cow. Chicken is chicken, unless it rooster. We no name animals. We no make friends with none of 'em except farm dog. He stays chained up cuz he want kill chickens. Once dog do that, he no good, ever! Then we get rid of dog." Grammom never mentioned exactly *how* she'd do *that*.

One day when I was barely five years old, I had my first message about the enormity awaiting me about life. It was just us two, sharing a quiet moment in the farmyard, Grammom and little-girl me.

"See this hen here," Antonina, born on a Lithuanian farm herself before the twentieth century began, before the Bolshevik Revolution and all hell broke out in Eastern Europe.

Antonina grabbed the hen she intended for our stew pot that evening. As she instructed, I stood in front of her, dazed and amazed at the sturdy stout woman. In one quick flash of her strong wrist, she twisted the hen's neck for its instantaneous death; then slash-slash gutted it with the sharp knife she always kept safely sheathed in her apron pocket. Then, with the chicken's innards steaming in that summer's cool morning, she looked up at her small charge and began to quietly explain to me, what in retrospect, I came to call— Grammom's Cosmic Truth. Standing hypnotically still, riveted to the spot, astounded and, to this day, I can clearly remember, more profoundly than any of the other reveals I've received from the Great Teachers I've worked with, the lesson this simple peasant grandmother of mine gave me: my first Big Shocking Realization.

"See this," Grammom said, "see her yolks here." She pointed at the bright bloody mess inside the slain hen, to what looked like a fireworks cluster of varying sizes of bright yellow balls surrounded by runny redness. The pungent smell of warm fresh chicken blood overwhelmed me. I felt weak in the knees, but solidly upright, fascinated at the same time. Amid the gore, I saw it. The sacrificed bird's inner cluster of brilliant yellow yolks—some, not-yet-laid but ready, big and fully formed, ready to drop, and other yolks tiny, not-nearly-ready to drop, and every size in between—were attached to one another like a bundle of garish, lemon-colored carnival balloons, held together by an invisible string. "These, all eggs chicken ever make in her life, all here, always here, inside her. If I'd a let her live. But ... she happy to be our dinner tonight. That her job, chicken job, being our food."

Dumbstruck I stood, in eyes-wide alarm. Not shocked, in awe. I stood silently in reverent, breathtaking awe. Witnessing this strong magic Grammom was making right before me. I felt like I was being sucked right into the middle of that cluster of steamy wet, pungent, dead chicken-smelling yellow yokes—swarming in the middle of the blood-red and darkened-black guts, swirling shapes of pinks, blues, greens, a choking rainbow of colors and strong odors overpowering me. I floated away, transported to some other place, some other time.

As I stared at the chaotic, scary innards before me, listening to Grammom, I saw, in what felt like a momentary flash, the beginning-middle-and-end of all that ever was, is, and will ever be.

The hen's insides revealed, in its vibrant yellow yolks, the entire cosmos spinning before my eyes. It was all I'd need to know about the natural order of things, thanks to Grammom's showing me; her few garbled utterances, her gesturing guidance, without any fancy words of explanation. In that brief moment, little-girl me understood that death is nothing but part of life. And life is renewed, like each sacrificial yard bird's yokes that would have fallen from its cluster when ripened, one by one, to be made into another hard-crusted egg once its soft liquified shell hit the air outside. Food, nourishment for another of God's creatures—over and over—until the yellow yokes, like a million little yellow universes, each of them with a purpose, got used up. Then the hen's life too, would end (if it had escaped Grammom's pot) because its life purpose would be completed, when every last one of its eggs got dropped. The eggs, the purpose of the hen's existence, are *all there*, from the beginning of its laying life up to when the very last one drops.

Ben, the old farm dog, chained to its tree-shaded house, looked longingly on, licking his chops, thinking how delicious that stinking-dead chicken would be, if it were dropped into his mouth, not in the human's cook pot.

Years later, I would realize what happened to me on that day, when my height barely reached my grandmother's waist. When I was shown the first, the only insight I'd ever need, into the natural and eternal order of things. A simple lesson from my simple farmer Grammmom. I didn't know what profound knowledge Grammmom imparted to me that day. All I knew was that I trusted her beyond measure. Everything she said and did, I readily absorbed. She was the truest, most honest, most real of all people I'd ever met. She loved to sit under the heavy-with-fruit plum tree outside her farmhouse screen door, and let me brush her waist-long hair, usually pinned up tightly in a no-frills bun all day. We'd sit quietly and drink some freshly cooled milk from that morning's milking. That's when Grammmom laughed the most, telling me strange Baltic fairy tales as I softly brushed and brushed her soft silky hair.

Then Antonina gathered her apron around her firm stout form, pinned her hair up in one swift move, and said, "Now we feed pigs, Linduta!" And off the two of us went, to the face-slapping strong-smelling pen where the muddy swine squealed in delight at the sight of us approaching.

As a grown up, I was visiting a local New Hampshire farm with friends. From atop a hill, our small group looked down upon the farmyard's star, a substantial pig named, of all things, Hermione. The owners of the farm were French, and this was a common name back in their small village in Haute Provence.

We stood on the hilltop talking softly, my host explaining the farm's gentile equal-to-all organic approach to rural life. Practically the opposite from my grandparents, "Let's survive best we can by eating everything we grow" farm ethic I'd been raised on.

"We simply couldn't butcher her, when she reached the proper size," the husband said about Hermione, who was curled up in a mounded ball of pink in the farmyard, far below us.

"She was too adorable. And she'd become our pet. We simply couldn't think about eating her," the wife explained.

"Yes, we both love our dear *Hermione!*" they exclaimed in

unison.

At the sound of her own name, down the hill from where our group stood looking at the pig, we saw the insanely oversized animal instantly pick up her resting head, her ears pointing straight up skyward. Hearing her name, the monstrously oversized pig looked behind her and saw her beloved human parents standing with some others. As if hearing a cue from inside her head, Hermione quickly stood up on her tiny, delicate back hoofs and raised her spindly front legs—and began to dance! We humans roared in delight, shouting, "Hermione! Hermione!" Her midget feet barely looked like they could support her girth, which had to be hundreds of pounds more than she ought to have weighed. Not only was she dancing on two legs but, I laughed aloud thinking, "How could this be?" the gargantuan pig started spinning in a circle, all the while looking up at our group for approval, acknowledgement—more adoration—on every pirouette, for one, two, three complete spins on her back pinpricks of her teensy hoofed feet. Her sight's fixation on her audience seemed purely from Hermione's sheer delight in her dance, performed for our delirious pleasure, executed with practiced finesse.

We all laughed at such silliness! Hermione dancing! High above the barnyard I stood gazing at this bizarre sight below, dazzled, mesmerized by a pig, once again. For quite a few minutes Hermione twirled this way and that, performing as if her life depended on dancing her little heart right out of that overgrown, blubbery body of hers.

Spinning and hopping around, up on her two spindly pin legs, never looking like this was either a bother or an effort, she was a dervish, an elephantiasis Miss Piggy, dancing, twirling in Sufi ecstasy. She was the lead ballerina in Tchaikovsky's *Swine Lake*, extending herself beautifully, elegantly pointing hoof and nose in a well-executed glissade, glancing up the hill to make sure her captivated audience still held her in their focus.

Until the clapping and laughter of the viewers overwhelmed

her, and she finally came to rest. Standing on all fours, panting, her head held high in a salute of love, respect, and … could this actually be one of her thoughts? It surely looked like it … Hermione truly acted as if she felt the equality of her piggyness with our humanness.

Just then the wife on this "gentleman's farm" (as "farms for pleasure" are called) turned to her guests and said with a smile.

"This is why Pierre and I have decided our next set of piglets simply *must be named* Breakfast, Lunch, and Dinner. It's ridiculous, we know, to have such an enormous beast as our pet. But Hermione will be our dear pig family-member until the day she dies, naturally."

It's an interesting time, this crossroads of homespun American purity mixing with the rash of our nation's current power-hungry control freaks who, for far too long, have abused women, children, and other men too. The nature of a revolution is: it starts with outrage.

Ultimately, we all have to help each other to feel safe in the skin-suit we are born with. Whether we're born part of humankind, or an equal-status barnyard animal, we all deserve to live our lives as happily, as stress-free as we can. No matter what species we happen to be, we want to feel safe and able to trust our surroundings.

The extremes that go along with a radical shift in society's group consciousness, such as the exposure of sexual abuse currently is, mirrors the inward Self-reflection needed for spiritual growth. It's the scourge of so-called civilization, some of us know, to ignore our animal natures and our need to be in relationship with Nature It-Self. I can admit I'm no angel. Earlier in life I'd abused myself and perhaps a few others (some old boyfriends would readily attest); the result, I have no doubt today, of perpetuating the pattern of being disconnected from Spirit, as I was back then.

Abuse causes more abuse, until awareness breaks in and the Light of knowledge shines onto the darkness of ignorance. When the

Light penetrates the fog of forgetfulness, then consciousness grows.

I trust that my fellow humans are trying to get better, one person at a time, all at our different paces. Yet until the world starts talking publicly about spiritual awakenings as well as sexual improprieties, and faces the fact that controlling others, whether sexually or by other too common and cruel methods—things will remain stagnant in the evolutionary department for closed-minded individuals. But for us hybrid vigors, we are already in a sea change of uplifted consciousness.

That change is about each of us evolving, heightening our awareness, and committing to living as hybrid vigors.

Breath by breath, person by person, the awareness that is possible for an individual to experience higher ways of thinking and feeling—usually starts with a shock! A grossly inappropriate en-counter with another person is enough to force-start the transfor-mation of a person wanting to, no, *needing* to elevate themselves. Everyone wants to let loose of others controlling their level of happiness.

We are everywhere, we awakening hybrid vigors. And human-kind is, as a result, becoming more spiritually aware with each little bit of control-or-be-controlled that gets loosened from our human condition.

Rejoice in the freedoms we enjoy now. Each of us, women, men and in-betweens, we are sexually liberated, all genders, Free At Last! Enjoy spiritual sex, that most divine of human pleasures, with any others whom you choose to share your most sacred, most powerful creative energies.

CHAPTER 18

a love worth living for

Adog often senses things going wrong before anything actually happens. That's why certain breeds, notably Weimaraner and golden retrievers, are so sensitive that they are used as seizure-alert dogs for people suffering from epilepsy or have severe allergies. Like many animals, canines uncannily sense the approach of an earthquake, tsunami, and other natural catastrophes before their imminent strike becomes detectable even by sensitive scientific instruments. Many dogs' sixth sense is so powerful they can smell cancer growing in a person's body long before a diagnosis has been made.

In ancient times, temples and holy places were guarded by wolf-like jackals for the Egyptians, Rottweilers for the Romans, and chows for the Chinese Empires. In myth, both the Norse and Persians spoke of four-eyed, and the Greeks, three-headed dogs that guarded their versions of the underworld. Since the beginning of recorded history, stories of this sensitivity of canines proves their ability to discern a true seeker from a thief, whenever a stranger approached sanctums of higher knowledge. For the reason of unparalleled loyalty, Dog was chosen to guard the sacred temples.

One of the distinctions between cat people and dog people is … if a cat bites, it often gets infected; whereas a dog's mouth has an antibiotic quality to it that makes infections clear up—if you're lucky enough to get your sores licked by a slobbering, friendly dog.

A complete stranger of a dog rescued me once. A savior, who

just happened to be passing by as I was lying on a friend's sofa, lost in one of those dark demonic places my not-yet-awakened self used to fall into. Somehow—I'd fallen into another deep hellish well of paralyzing fear, that, at the time, was part of my life's unsteady plight, another reason why I'm so freaking grateful to have gotten out of mental torment.

It was a balmy summer evening, back then. The doors had been thrown wide open onto the Cape Cod beach, whose waves I could hear from the living room where I lay alone on a couch, silently writhing in unspeakable mental anguish. My eyes were clenched shut. I remember experiencing psychic pain so severe that I distinctly thought I was dying right then. Perhaps what I suffered might be called a panic attack, but just then it felt like death was pulling me down down *down*, to its dark abyss.

Suddenly—without realizing I'd sunk so dangerously deep into this emotional chasm—I was startled to feel a wet coldness touch my fingers, which dangled over the side of the sofa.

My clenched eyes burst opened at the wetness—and I stared right into the warm sparkling brown eyes of a completely strange yellow dog, whose moist snout was pushing at my hand as if saying, "Hey! Snap out of it!" The unknown dog's eyes remained riveted on mine as he or she kept pushing, pushing my hand—trying to help me out of the self-made pit I'd fallen into. The dog startled me right out of my despair. And by holding fast onto its reassuring gaze s/he completely pulled me out of that wretched pit I was in. Somehow this dog jolted me out of my self-absorbed state of torture. Looking right into the dog's eyes, its huge furry face looming over me, I swore I heard a voice saying aloud, "What you're feeling is just in your mind. Wake Up! You're safe! There's nothing to be afraid of! Relax. Breathe easy. I'm here for you. I love you."

The rescue dog stayed with me until my rapid breathing returned to normal, my heartbeat softened … to normal, and … I must have dozed off.

When I awoke the dog was gone. Never to be seen or heard of again. And no one at the house I was staying at had ever seen this dog who saved me, not before, not during its rescue mission, and never afterwards, either.

Over the next few years a few more incidents happened in which I found my mind sinking, once again, into that self-inflicted abyss of Darkness. I had to learn how to crawl out of it on my own. Each time, I relied on repeating the life-altering lesson that golden dog had taught me.

It's only in my mind, I'd repeat silently, whenever I felt myself sinking into the dangerous riptide of self-centered fear, the kind of fear that has no real basis, no actual source, nothing but … memory.

Each time it returns, I remember what my angel dog had said to me, through its eyes. And each time the nameless horror struck, the pain level lessened. To be perfectly honest, I still get a remnant of this familiar panic, but only when I'm on the verge of falling asleep. Today I know how to soothe myself (I repeat my sacred mantra till I fall asleep), reminding myself, *It's only in my mind*, just like the mystery golden dog did for me, so long ago.

"It's only your mind, this awfulness that seems real," I heard my miracle dog silently comfort me that day. Still, the memory of my former fucked-upness, my childhood brokenness, perhaps, or a memory left over from another lifetime, who knows. But it tries to trip me up, to this day. As I fall asleep, a decades-long sober and happily spiritualized hybrid vigor, I remind myself, repeating as many times as I have to until sleep overtakes me:

You're not dying; you're alive! Focus on your breath; you are breath itself. Your breath is the Source of Life. That other stuff, that's just your mind playing tricks on you, you fool.

In time, I grew to love this part of myself more than anything in the world, the part within me that is synonymous with Bliss, the higher form of my Self. Trusted teachers eventually showed me that this part of who I am is what some call *God consciousness*, and the key to making it mine, as often and as near as I wished, is to tune into the very breath that's within me. I began to experience, for real, that the Light is within me, too. And that completely changed my outlook about things.

I love that the word *inspiration* means exactly that: to be filled with Spirit ... to breathe Spirit in ... because that's what it feels like *to be inspired*. When I'm being still, and do nothing other than follow the in- and out-breath of my natural breathing, everything else—all of life's many complexities, complete and utter weird-nesses—dissolves, when I follow the steady rhythm of my own relaxed breathing.

Before that blond dog rescued me, it was me who'd been letting my own imagined fear freak me out for far too long.

Heaven and hell, gods and goddesses, deities of all dimensions, they are only so many fairy tales to help explain the Divine con-nection between my relaxed, higher Self and my breath. When I found that sweet spot, deep within my own quietude—I could worship the Eternal Stillness within, because, at last, I could feel *It*. Then I could see *It* within everything and everybody else as well.

Of all belief systems—myths and stories that we humans keep telling ourselves, to help us to relax and enjoy life so we can sleep more comfortably at night, and help bring some order to the chaos of worldly existence—enjoy which one works best for you. When a belief stops working, know that you can choose to go within your own Self, learn to silently listen to your own breathing ... and you will always know great peace.

My job is to continue to tell everyone who listens:

First we save our own ass; bring peace to our own life; however we do this doesn't matter. Consider yourself blessed if you are among the people who experience true inner peace, if even for a short while. After you attain this *peace that passes all under-standing*, be sure to spread it to the rest of your brothers and sisters.

The world's leaders, of faiths, of political systems, and all other types of chiefs among our tribes, they must spiritualize their view of life here on earth—so their followers will, in due course, achieve peace, too. Inner peace is absolutely necessary in order to serve the continuation of human civilization. Inner peace comes first to any individual who chooses to have it, and then world peace can happen, naturally and organically, person by person. The more people who've done the inner work of remembering who and what we are, the more peace will be in the world. In a peaceful state, we will be open-minded enough to receive workable solutions that arise in the collective unconscious, to solve our environmental and any other kinds of challenges that ever face us, today and in the future.

The world, the living goddess the ancients called Gaia, needs each of its children to stop obsessing about their personal problems. Dissolve your fears. Take up waving the courageous banner of compassionate love to address yours first, so we can together, heal the planet's problems. Whatever one's challenges may be, inner peace can be attained. Visualize a yellow angel dog, or a cat, a pet pig or rabbit, any animal as a totem to help heal your inner Self. Let your personal totem love you back to wholeness. Let your animal-guide's presence, or an Unseen, if you prefer, help re-set your aching heart.

I've been asked by my inner guide to relay the Light of Hope available to all of us. With humility, I am playing the role of my Unseen's reporter, here:

Noname says: "All atrocities of humans needing to control other humans will be eradicated when Spirit, the energy of Universal Love, is acknowledged as the true Source of existence that invisibly connects us, all as One. Humankind is One. One opened-minded, big-hearted person linked to the next by the most powerful force of Life, the invisible flowing energy—of Love."

Adversity makes us become better people, once we survive its wrath. Without fire's tempering, metal cannot find its true tensile strength. Fire is needed to eliminate dross from gold, and impurities from ghee, just as each of us must experience the discomfort and distress needed to initiate Self-awareness. Know that this fire of purification within our human psyche is also the impetus that forces us to grow ever closer to who and what we are. We are Divinity wearing numerous body suits. We humans are the Army of Love.

This fire of purification is what I had to go through, in order to free myself from the soul-restraints of my life's previous pitfalls. I willed myself to leave my damaged little self behind. Gaining strength through tests of emotional cleansing brought me to a place where I could access my inner wisdom, helping to heal the sadness of my life. Just as I had to go through the psychic "fire" that leads to wisdom to reach this place of inner peace, humankind is also going through the fire of purification as a society, as a global blended family, which includes all other life forms, and Gaia's earthly belongings, which includes the land, the sea and sky surrounding our garden planet.

Our personal fires are the emotional, mental, or physical distresses we are each called upon to deal with. Each of us must battle our own demons by ourselves. Or let an occasional rescue-dog, person or teacher help you, when they appear offering guidance. As a family of blended humans, we citizens of the world need to transform our personal fears into Love, so we can then affect real world-healing action.

A family suffers when even one of its members is suffering from a dis-ease. As long as fear resides in the human heart, Love must be publicly and loudly proclaimed, in order to offset the undesirable effects that man-made fear will do, if left unchecked.

In pre-hybrid vigor time, when either a certain being or an entire fragment of society had been determined by *others* to have unacceptable traits, or an infected spirit; that is, when someone was found not to fit into the criteria of a particular belief-system's, agreed-upon *civilized norms*—the *unacceptable* outcasts were either taken to the priest, rabbi, Imam, or an indigenous tribe's shaman, to be exorcised, shunned or ignored, or, in extreme cases, banished or exterminated through social alienation or senselessly violent ritual acts.

Now, with hybrid vigors re-birthing ourselves left and right, a new solution is available for the crisis of our out-of-balance humans' survival on planet Earth.

Those of us who are already awakened are helping others who haven't yet been uplifted, haven't yet *chosen to open* their closed hearts and *be* a hybrid vigor. The world's population of *enlightened* versus *not-yet* is soon to far out-number our old species, the homo sapiens, with their closed minds and rusted-shut hearts.

Homo sapiens has already proven itself a nonfunctioning, soon-to-be-extinct version of what our true potential is. We hybrid vigors know we are the true hope of our world's future. We are living for Love.

Love is the *Wake Up!* cold wet nose of our universal rescue dog. The creative energy of Love is our only hope to transform our terminally sick world into a viable healthy environment in which we can continue evolving as the sensitive, thinking, speaking race of hominoids we are so fortunate to be born as.

Colonizing Mars is pie-in-the-sky futile wishfulness as a solution for the survival of all humanity. Wherever the old form of civilized humankind finds itself, fear-based folks will fall victim to the dis-ease of separation that homo sapiens has convinced itself is the only reality.

The Unseen Spirit of Love is a part of the material world, as much as our physical bodies are.

The old must make way for the new.

The time is here.

Lovers of Spirit have a moral obligation to repair any weak link in the interconnected *Army of Love*, my name for our self-birthed, *trans*formed human family of hybrid vigors. Psychologists and psychiatrists tell us how young people are so confused about gender issues, an ever-increasing phenomenon in human society. As loving members of our blended family of humankind, acceptance of this trend of *trans* and other kinds of social fluidity, includes respecting spiritual and religious, as well as gender-identity freedoms. It's not just a person's freedom to choose their sexuality, or the end of sexual discrimination that needs to shift. Today, a spiritual kind of *trans*, a person's inner *trans-formation* has been awakened, and is being craved-for in record number. When it comes to issues about whatever is most important to each of us, we must demand creative freedom for all, to fully embrace a hybrid-vigor style of Love.

Hybrid vigors re-birthing themselves—on the spot some-times—happens in all forms and formless manifestations. Our thoughts create; our minds build. Every action begins with a thought; a choice is made then, whether we're conscious of having made it, or not. Our arm obeys the brain to reach out for a coffee cup; it doesn't reach out on its own accord. The presence of the Unseen dimension, the invisible, golden-messengers of expanded consciousness, are influencing us HVs everywhere one looks. Wide-eyed, open-hearted, open-minded, kind acceptance is proof of the arrival, at long last, of *homo spiritus*, taking over from the old, broken reality-system of the material-only belief of before. More and more homo sapiens *can* let go and let G-o-d: embracing the Good-Orderly-Direction of expanded, heightened consciousness that's waiting to be acknowledged within each newly awakened, re-birthed human soul.

With the survival of our blended human family happening, one-person-at-a-time, hybrid vigors look around and see what needs to be changed. And do it—one small change at a time.

Having started with transforming our own inner selves, we head out into the world and help others to change, bit by bit, act by act, kindness upon kindness. Respectful attitudes replace demoralizing debasement of a world whose collective soul so sorely needs a *trans*plant.

The Army of Love is filled with infinitely abundant and eager souls who are waiting to reveal themselves, to help our human family grow ever more expansive in possibilities. With our interconnected, awakened minds and our unlocked hearts—all things are possible.

Believe in miracles!

Loyal to the greater good, no matter what, all hybrid vigors are very much like rescue dogs. Hybrid vigors know the human family is in a state of high distress; we are not in denial. Juvenile suicide is the highest, ever. The world is a confusing, complex place, for many. Yet we HVs remain ever hopeful, willing to help, reaching out to any in fear, giving hugs and words of encouragement and other Wake Up! *wet licks* wherever they're needed, just like the unknown golden dog did who came to rescue me.

Humankind has come a long way since its cave dwelling and hunter-gatherer origins. Our life spans have increased for good reason: there's a lot of work for us to do.

God is so big, *It* cannot be contained in a single religion, or defined by any one name like "Spirit," or be limited by one rigid belief system that excludes others. Each of us must discover answers for ourselves about the most mysterious thing of life, the greatest of all Mysteries: the Light of consciousness within. I still prefer calling *It*, Love.

CHAPTER 19

shit happens – so hold on!

Arising from Roostie's stretched-out throat each dawn, each dusk, and at random times throughout any given day—his call is heard, and with it comes a thrilling sense of expectation.

Roostie's call for awakening can come at any time, night or day.

Like anything else that is part of minute-by-minute daily life—Roostie's call becomes, like one's own breath, something one doesn't think much about anymore. His awakening screech so constantly occurring has made it ... normal.

The normalcy of this time of change we're in right now, of humanity's evolutionary transformation, is as much a part of every-day life as Roostie's random calls of awakening.

These boisterous calls of *Attention!* have become a part of the natural order of things. So, when we hear Roostie's robust reminders we oftentimes ... don't get moved by the alarming, but now unspecified, at-all-times sound of his screeching. The blasted barnyard cawing that once might have annoyed us, or awoken us, has now blended into the background of all the other ambient noise of life that barrages us, constantly, because Roostie lives—every-where! Screens always aglow and speaking; talking heads texting, face-timing, phoning; cars-trucks-trains-planes passing, insects buzzing, birds exuberantly calling, people demanding, sirens alerting us loud-to-louder, then fading till ... gone.

What was once supernatural, Roostie's bizarre male chicken

alerts, have now become natural to us. His Wake Up! calls, a regular, wonder-filled fixture of our many sense-experiences, just as the spectacular display of majestic clouds above, so often goes unnoticed by us.

Now, when Roostie calls, whether from way off in the distance or from up close, face-to-face personal—do any of us pay attention? When he reminds us there's work to do?

Roostie's job is to remind us of our limitations. That we don't have to accept them. That we can change them, if we want to.

Roostie's marvelously operatic feat, his throat fully strained, reminds us, over and over, that we are ready to step into the realm of Being—not wishing to become, but—BEing a hybrid vigor.

Last week was really rough.

I hate to admit it, but for the first time in years, I found myself licking the disgusting inside rim of the super nasty pity pot. I was besieged by an unexpected bout of ugly business: soul puke. Disappointments, people conflicts, misunderstandings, rejections, heartbreaks, they all lined up in a row and waved their battle flags over my battered, worn-out carcass. My tried-and-true resiliency got severely tested, gory details thankfully withheld. So what did I do? I indulged. Not something I'm proud of but, hey!—I'm human, and yes, I am a hybrid vigor type human. Most times, this still-neophyte hybrid vigor-ness of mine feels pretty balanced, but last week—I lost it. Momentarily, I forgot that I'm a committed hybrid vigor. Utterly ignoring everything I've shared with you, I ate all the sugar I could get my hands on. Sadly, I let my commitment unravel, to my own health, healing, and happiness, not to mention forgetting about helping to uplift my brothers and sisters. I'm embarrassed, but feel compelled to reveal the utter depths, which I allowed myself to sink. Last week my old "I'm not good enough" refrain returned. Instead of invigorating Self Love, I fell backwards, flat onto my former bad-news little self.

To hell with this self-birthing crap! Uplifting, hybrid shy-brid, vigor/schmig-or. This consciousness thing be damned!

What could possibly have caused such a backslide, you wonder? Two steps forward, a million backwards? All of us know the way progress goes, of any sort, for any worthwhile endeavor.

It could have been anything, that's how fragile we humans are. The false feeling of failure can be triggered by something as simple as tripping over a pebble and bruising a toe, or something so large as losing a loved one. Getting a speeding ticket. Someone looking at me funny. Someone forgetting to say "Hi." Someone weird saying "Hi."

Facetious? Hardly.

We humans are so damn sensitive, our feelings all over the place, and unpredictable, that sometimes it seems anything can throw us off our centers, if we're not vigilant. Okay, we hybrid vigors are people who certainly try to improve our lot, our race, even. We're folks who are working on not being so blown around by the fickle winds of feelings-getting-hurt, confused or angry over the state of the world.

You'd think after all the practice I've had, I'd know better? Wrong!

Whoosh—I fell through the rabbit's hole of self-pity once again—! In this instance of forgetting who and what I am, I'm happy to report, I only fell back a wee bit. Only fell from Love Consciousness into a heap of bleeding-breathing, dried-up leather— for just a few short hours—instead of landing at the very bottom of that wormhole of confusion I used to frequent.

That familiar low, rough feeling, that shitty old nemesis of mine, self-pity. How I hate being there! I've climbed out of it now so I can admit the foible of my un-watchfulness, the reason I slipped from the brilliant throne of being Self Loving. So now, I'm admitting, *again*: I'm willing to accept my imperfections, my humanness because it's my imperfections that make me, well, perfectly *me*. Yes, there's a part of me that's Divine, that can touch the eyes and be the hand of God with my thoughts and my better choices. But for just a moment last week, I'd forgotten.

I forgot to honor how perfect in my imperfections I am, how we all are. Discovering and accepting our own shortcomings is part of our transformative path. Our imperfections help us discover our Source of contentment. I had forgotten how I must let my sober (true) feelings show me who I really am; and, however momentarily, I fell off the path of Self-awareness.

The ringing bells of the Voice within, my inner "Roostie," shout, "I'm ready! Bring on the Next Lesson I so badly need to get me where I'm supposed to go! Next *Insight,* all aboard for the return trip to bliss, my natural birthright!"

Even the best of us gets plundered by life events every now and then. And when shit happens—even the most "aware" person can easily forget the basic spiritual tools that help keep us safe and sane, healthy and … feeling easy in our skin. We're all going to lose it when it's our turn, as we journey together on the road less traveled.

Forgiving ourselves is the rank stripe we first earn in the Army of Love.

Noname, I typed as fast as I could think the words, *what do I need to focus on to get back in balance? I feel so off. So off center, off joy, off kilter, off everything. Bingeing on delicious treats has only made it worse; damn this pleasure-trap, this insatiable mouth I have!*

I'm ready to do what I need to right myself, to get myself back on track. To let go of life's disappointments, and once again take up the armor of being a lieutenant in the Army of Love. I forgot, for a little while there, to practice what turns me on the most, didn't I?

So I'm reminding myself, lovingly, right here. To accept life for what it is. To see God in each other, as wicked, wonderful, pathetic or inspiring as we might be. Higher Power consciousness chooses to appear in the collective human form, the Fellowship of Spirit: I accept this. I renew my promise to remember that all people are cells of Great Spirit, not just hybrid-vigor types. All in existence is connected to consciousness, even though I had forgotten that. I'm ready now, to get back to that place where I'm most comfortable. Accepting that All is exactly as it's meant to be, even things that sometimes appear as "wrong" or "bad" or "unjust."

The seas are toxic, the atmosphere is threatened, the ice caps are melting, and politicians and heartless corporations seem not to care a hoot.

There must be a reason for the challenges we meet along this journey. Choosing (or not choosing) to figure out the Enigma of Existence is the purpose of our great freedom, our free will. Saying this, I willingly choose to renew my membership as a hybrid vigor, again.

To respect and honor my Self, I know, is my number one job. I slipped and fell into the pit of feeling sorry for myself, because I forgot that maintaining a link with Love, forgot to trust that Love is all that's needed for change, for transformation. That's all. I momentarily forgot. I'm human, just like the time I lost it with the Muslim guy shouting at me in my own house. I remember now, that's all that matters. Now I can renew my pledge:

To forgive myself and all others. I accept that my being imperfect, is me being perfectly human. Being content with what happens even though one feels like shit, is the highest expression of Self Love: a state of mind in which we all begin and end our journey. Some call this the ego-less state, or mind-less-ness. Being content with What is.

I can accept that certain people, places and things hurt my heart more than I wished they did. My cousin committing suicide last week, really got my heartbeat up. All I can do is forgive. Forgive that he chose to off-himself instead of coping. I too, have let fear and confusion kill my spirit. But I'm better now, remembering, once again, that some things are beyond my ever knowing answers to.

I am, right here and now, re-focusing my efforts. Once again, I'm deciding to remain in my Big Heart, not my conflicted puny mind. Once the white sugar blues wears off and I've sweated out all the negative ions that have scratched and clawed their way into my body temple—I'm back on track.

Maybe next time, when so much bad news arrives all at once, I'll be stronger. At least I no longer worship the grape, or have to have a bad-girl fix. I'm grateful for these improvements in my interior-renovation.

Senseless violence all around, real-life or made-up—nerve- and blood-cringing movies, streaming or on TV; massacres, horrors, today's news—there's too much insanity out there.

We're a world gone mad!

Global warming, environmental pollution, glaciers melting, animals disappearing.

Breaking News terrorist attacks vying neck-to-neck with animals disappearing and crazy naked reality shows and video-game mortal combat, everything we hear, done in a form of *entertainment.*

Is art depicting life? Or is humanity's need for a living nightmare that never ends?

The Coliseum's murderous gladiator-instinct has gone viral.

If we don't cultivate peace *inside,* it just doesn't exist, period.

Booze and pharmacologicals are some people's mistaken way of shifting to pleasure mode, their best bet, most accessible and culturally-acceptable choice for the highest high a person can muster, a cheap substitute for inner peace: numbness.

Nothing works to bring about change, not enduringly, except the weapon of inner illumination. *One Love* as Bob Marley called *It,* is how to combat all of humanity's woes.

The labyrinth of keeping mind-body-spirit in balance … it takes vigilance to not get lost in the maze of constantly being barraged from numerous outside-, and for some of us, inner-demons, that continually stalk our well-earned inner peace.

As mentioned earlier, human feelings are *signs* for when we are being urged by the invisible energy of consciousness that unites us all. The Unseen *dimension* is just as much life's true reality as this solid bunch of words. Feelings of discomfort and un-ease come equally from visible and invisible forces that surround us, helping us to move us forward. The purpose of our feelings is to urge us to make changes, demanding we do *something*. Or else we'll surely experience emotional sickness, stuck-ness, and unhealthy sorrow. Feelings of wellness express satisfaction, contentment, and our reward is wholesome health. Stress shows us the need to rest, assimilate, and be more grateful for what we have in life: to stop and take a breather. No stress means: We have paid attention; we took a break. We *are aware* of our breathing. We never stay the same for very long. There is always a next step upward, just as there might be a surprise fall backward, as my slip back into the sugar-lined hole of addiction proved.

Stagnation, ennui, entropy are empty feelings all of us fall victim to. The more a person decides to get better, get happier (by being more useful to others), we hybrid-vigors-in-training need to be, especially, more kind to ourselves. We need to take breaks whenever feeling overwhelmed. Do something special for our Selves when we feel sad, drained, on low battery, and affected by any form of negativity.

This is what evolution is about. Expanding, contracting, never the same; outwardly and inwardly always perceiving, selecting that which works best for our own and humankind's survival. For me and for all other hybrid vigors, this means seeing the One that we are wherever we look, hear, taste, feel, see, or ... somehow, without knowing how or why, we oddly *sense* that unity we all really are. Developing the perception, the True perception, that we are united with *All That Is* ... this is the crowning glory of a hybrid vigor's efforts.

Feelings tell us how to turn, adjust, add to or take away whatever caused our lives to get out of whack. That's why the *feeling* part of life is essential. For those of us who still occasionally try to run from our feelings—as I did this last time when the shit hit the fan, big time, indulging in a don't-feel-anything binge, numbing my feelings with food instead of facing the loss and despair before me—we must remember to forgive our human nature that is prone to weakness. The perfectly natural, built-in imperfection we all possess makes us perfectly human.

That's why it's important to remember: feelings are *signs*. If we *listen to them*, not run or hide from or mask them (as mood- and mind-substances do), we can learn from our feelings. It's only people who tune out their feelings, as I used to do, that never get to know how blissful a balanced life, our natural animal-state, actually is.

Losing it last week showed me I'm not cured, I'm just a work-in-progress. I need to re-focus when I get overwhelmed from a barrage of negatives. I need to remember to focus on the healthier, happier positives of life. Like remembering to take a look up at the gorgeous clouds now and then. I've renewed my commitment to my hybrid vigor-ness now.

After three whopping big negatives hit me right between the eyes: the suicide in my family; my work slamming into yet another rejection hurtle; and the depressing state of the political divide and subsequent uneasiness that my country suffers presently; bam bam bam!—I weakened.

So big deal, for a few days I ate obsessively and plumped out, instead of shedding tears and whining a few symphonies of *Poor Me's*. But then I remembered. And I let my beloved Will, once again, act like the big comforting brother he is at times like these. I let him humor me back to loving myself. As spiritual mates, we comfort one another whenever we need. We've given our permission to help each other grow as close to Spirit as possible, especially when one of us is feeling low.

I get to do the same for Will when he's down. Ain't love grand! Being helpmates is another *added plus* besides the joy of spiritual sex in our life together.

Today, out of that uncomfortable, illogical self-pity pot, I realize I have more work to do. Sometimes my unease needs to ask a question … so I sit at my keyboard and type out Noname's response as I listen.

Noname says: "Limit your time with those who are chained to their anger, blame others, and wallow in victimhood. So many people, especially politicos, have become angry beyond reason. Understand their frustrations, but guard against psychic leaks in your limited amount of Life Force energy. Choose to creatively help look for new solutions to your society's problems. New creative ways to help uplift your fellow humans is needed now more than ever.

"Being depressed, disappointed, or sad is only energy-consuming. It serves no other purpose than to drain your resources. Guard, and treasure your life's limited energies. During heart-wrenching times, remember to fill Self up with more Love, surround your Self with loving, accepting friends—not more sweets or substances."

Our free will allows us to notice when our lives need more balancing. Choice in this *game of life* is the *trick* that helps us keep from getting off kilter. Choosing to know the Self within is the ultimate purpose of human feelings. That takes constant effort. And that's exactly why some people are allergic to expanding their perceptions and prefer to stay numb with booze, pills, shopping, and other distractions. It's better to pay attention to how we feel, with whom we feel best, and let our feelings guide us to a happier way of being.

By now all of you realize that this "inner wisdom" I refer to is that part of our true nature, our Higher Self, our Divinity that being human entails. We have access to this inner guidance system at any time. The Unseen energy, or personal angel, if you prefer *that*, or whatever one wishes to call the assistance of a higher perspective we have *within* us—we always have access to *It* whenever we need, or want.

My *slip backwards* was just another opportunity, when it was over. I ended up recognizing the opportunity I had for more growth that those low feelings had brought me. More letting-go I had to do. And most likely, always will.

This last self-pity dunking might not be my last, but the lengths in between them are getting longer. I'm getting better. As a result of my quick rebound these days, insights I get about the Self within us all are getting more specific. Here's the one I received most recently.

I recognize that change is the name of the *Game of Life*. Change is the only constant there is, other than having faith in the Divine aspect of Life It-Self. Change is part of *nothing's forever*. Everything's made up of potential or real chaos. Change is, as much as Love, part of the universal consciousness that we are all part of.

Change is the plaintive cry of Roostie's awakening call—that comes from all directions at anytime, anywhere—even if we can't hear it when he's too far away, or gone entirely.

Some of us are Change-makers, compelled to share the joy of being alive, just for the unparalleled and true delight of how good it feels to hear and say these words aloud. Joy. Being Alive.

... before our hearts have opened

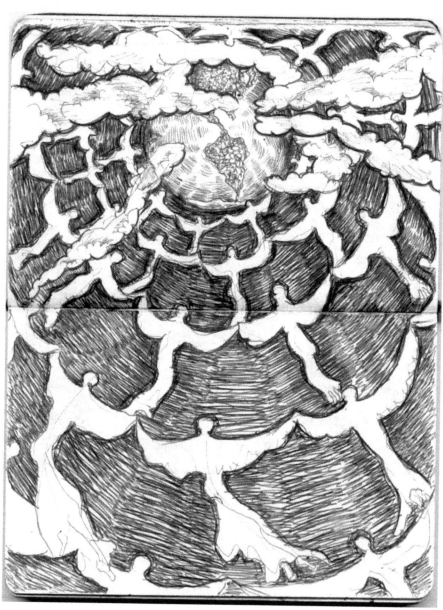

... after our hearts open ...

CHAPTER 20

the party (and religion) of love

One who is able to withdraw the senses, just as a tortoise withdraws its limbs, is established in divine wisdom.

Bhagavad Gita 2:58

Many widespread cultures began understanding themselves better by focusing on Turtle. From earliest Chinese legends, to Native American Peoples of many different Nations (or tribes), Turtle is famously noted in ancient civilizations for its steady wisdom, its tenacity and stable imperviousness to outside influences. Everyone knows how hard it is for a dome-shaped turtle to upright its own self. With its feet sturdily placed upon the earth, its shell impenetrable to most of its dangerous prey, this reptile outsmarts adversity by withdrawing when things get tough. The faster, mischievously cunning rabbit—noted in the ancient Greek Aesop's fable, the Hare and the Tortoise—loses to turtle; just as the reptile outdoes the high-flying crane in the Sumerian legend of the Heron and the Turtle. Mythical creatures of ancient China with abilities to go within, by asking and receiving wisdom, are collectively alluded to in the pantheon known as *the Four Entities that Possess Spirit*: the white tiger, the dragon, the phoenix, and … the magical turtle.

Turtle is the archetypal creature that best represents every human's ability to carry life's heavy burdens, endlessly, without complaint, without stopping … until every person's (or culture's) long-held goal has been reached. Turtle slowly and surely presses on, facing insurmountable obstacles, one after the next, until its quest is achieved. Steadily, step by step, it moves in an easy-going, unstressed manner, ever forward.

From earliest times, forms of Eastern deities have appeared in the turtle form. Vishnu—the Preserving force of the Hindu pantheon that includes, beside himself, Brahma and Shiva—historically reveals his Divinity as a small, trudging Turtle whenever there's been times of great crisis on Earth, symbolically demonstrating how the steady wisdom of that animal is capable of restoring the cosmic equilibrium. Ancient peoples of far different places and cultures from each other, have used the image of an unstoppable turtle to symbolize the need of humans to understand our origins, as well as our purpose of existence.

In North America, Native American Indians have always called their sacred land, *Turtle Island*, which to them is nothing less than *all land*, While East Indians even today, continue to portray a small insignificant turtle in sacred art as *The Messenger*. In paintings, bas-reliefs and sculptures, the puny, indestructible reptilian portrays the Divine's *impervious nature*, and is often depicted alongside a main deity revealed as an anthropomorphic god. Both animal-messenger and godlike preserver of existence, Turtle represents equally important aspects of the Divine to Easterners.

From the world over, stories as diverse as from early Judaism and Islam refer to Turtle similarly, just as the rock carvings of prehistoric North and South American Indians, and written myths of Eastern Hindus have done. The latter were written down in scripture such as the Bhagavad Gita, in which each deity (truly, an *Unseen* represented by either images or words) portrays various sacred aspects of a highly evolved human nature, male or female or in-between.

To include Turtle as a major figure in the creation myth of cultures so diverse as the ancient Egyptians' hieroglyphics, and the Native American Iroquois' oral history of storytelling, signifies that both incredibly disparate civilizations, honored and revered this reptile that signified longevity, wisdom, and most important of all— the nonviolent path of a peaceful, easy-going existence.

A turtle does not engage in conquest, battle, or tries to control anything. It lives solely to survive. Interestingly, most turtles live notoriously long lives. Nearly three hundred years old, giant turtles enjoy the bright sun on their hard carapaces, whether journeying overland in all environs but icy ones, or traveling thousands of miles tirelessly, via oceanic currents.

Marine turtles rush to the surf's edge as hatchlings, and then spend their entire lives in the sea. Mature females only return to land to lay their eggs; mature males return only when sick or dying.

Their hatchlings must be protected *from* and *by* us in order to have a chance of not dying before they reach the sea where, in addition to cars on the beach and pollution possibly killing them, they face the threat of being eaten by one of their natural predators. Vehicles must be restricted on beaches to avoid running over the inch-long creatures. Likewise, bright lights disorient the newly-hatched critters, making them crawl to their certain deaths in the opposite direction from the sea. If they are not protected by us humans, sea turtles surely will perish.

It's our turn now, to be the best we can be. We are stewards of the land and sea and all of Earth's creatures. It's pay-back time! Time for us to defend all other creatures from harm; they have acted as inspiration, guiding and protecting us as animal totems to our more primitive forebears for eons before this present day.

Turtle is symbolic of an endangered species that relies upon humans to nurture it, and by our doing so, we ensure its very existence. It is our sacred duty to protect all critters, big and small, but especially turtles, because so many of humanity's myths include this amphibious reptile in its creation stories.

Turtle has had profound worldwide influence on human society. Three stylistic, stacked land turtles make up the entirety of the flag's design for the small Lithuanian town of Seirijai; two turtles hold up the official crest for Ascension Island's government seal; a giant land tortoise is resplendent on green grass with a sole palm tree, on the Republic of Seychelles' Coat of Arms. Children of various worldwide traditions still hear their forebears' pagan mythology at storytelling time, when parents and grandparents relay legends about magical turtles portraying the challenge of life, in its most basic of attributes: perseverance. Often in those tales, Turtle plays the role of an inadvertent, passive hero who steadfastly depicts the triumph of goodness over evil, patience outweighing over-confidence; and children love how Turtle's steadfast benevolence wins over speedy, selfish braggarts.

In many origin fables, Turtle represents the defender of all that is good, taking right action. During stressful times, this is often depicted as withdrawing inwardly, as Turtle does. Some folk tales of Turtle show how the smartest humans learn to emulate the wise persistence of these sacred animals. Turtle survives in the harshest of conditions, from super arid deserts to the world's endless reaches of its watery regions. Sea turtles, land tortoises, or amphibious terrapins, all are emblems of survival and ingenuity, their self-protecting skills depicted in folklore as surpassing other critters' dexterity, strength, and trickery.

We humans would benefit more from mimicking Turtle's skill of practicing patience, and going within, especially in times of strife. A turtle's superior skills of survival are not as evident as, say, an attacking shark's more aggressive lethalness; or a menacing, bloodthirsty tiger about to pounce; or the fearsomeness of a snorting, stomping, raging bull; or the deadliness of a rattlesnake's painful strike. The long-suffering patience of Turtle is, nonetheless, paramount to success. Turtle is always portrayed as the unsuspecting winner in every situation.

Slow, steady, sure: Turtle keeps plodding toward its goal, marching to an inner drumbeat, ever onward on its course, drawn to its target like a splinter of metal is drawn to a magnet.

In Taoist art the tortoise represents the triad of earth, humankind, and heaven. Turtle says, "Never look back," because ... it simply can't. Its eyes are forever focused on the next step right in front of its nose. Always looking forward, it plods ahead, undeterred; in the end, outsmarting, outpacing, outliving every other creature. Native American Indians believe the cosmic tree of life emerges from the spine of the tortoise. That's why we all live on Turtle Island, planet Earth. According to the creation myth of the indigenous Ancient Ones. Turtle is the most respected of emissaries from Great Spirit.

Turtle withdraws into its protective shell when threatened. It hisses if disturbed, waits, watches, reserving its strength, relying on water and energy stored in its very flesh for emergency survival—until the time of safety finally arrives and normal life can once again be resumed.

A biologist friend of mine has been funded by the U.S. Government to study desert tortoises for decades, they are that important to understand, for humankind's future. Turtle's survival is a clue to how we humans need to adapt our abilities to survive the harshest conditions that might beset our world, either from man-made or naturally occurring disasters, or changes in weather patterns.

According to primitive African lore, Turtle is the cleverest wild animal of them all. Surpassing the mighty roar of the savannah's lion; the stampeding threat of the scrubland's elephant; the chest pounding thunder of the mighty mountain gorilla. Turtles are able to penetrate barriers that migrating whales, stampeding buffalo and other giant creatures on the rampage get stopped by. Smaller turtles can bypass any barrier as they methodically, slowly proceed to their goal with nothing in mind but their final destination. No barrier stops Turtle—not gigantic cliffs, nor rocky crevasses—nothing, except its own demise.

Digging with shovel-like front claws, gopher tortoises in the southeast U.S., where I live, burrow horizontally twenty, thirty feet into the earth, providing shelter and protection for an array of other creatures residing in this hot humid place. Compassionately, Turtle allows other animals to share its tunnel's protection from the weather, where peacefully, friends and enemies cohabit, all gratefully residing in the comfortable home of one lone gopher host. Here, each hard-shelled landlord rests among a crowd of poisonous and nonpoisonous snakes, side by side with rats and mice, weasels, gophers, foxes, possums, scorpions, spiders and ants and countless other insects ... all species welcome in Turtle's spaciously crafted abode of peace: its long, cool, spacious and safe tunnel.

Indeed, some people believe that Turtle—not the big-maned lion, and certainly not us spear-and- bomb-flinging humans—is the surprisingly lackluster, but ever-reliable *Big-Hearted King of the animal world.*

We're all here just for a while, visiting on Turtle Island, this life-supporting blue planet that whirls in space. All animals, of whatever species, are inter-related; we're all sentient beings of some lower or higher form, mobile or immobile. Earth's life forms are all more alike than different, all of us sharing surprisingly high percentages of mutually-similar DNA.

When I left the U.S. to protest the Vietnam War, living as an ex-pat in the West Indies for an entire decade, I found my re-entry to the States very difficult. During one of my visits home, my fellow Americans were in the middle of what looked to me, like a country-wide melt-down. The Watergate scandal, with its ensuing presiden-tial mess, was in the final stage of eruption. People were walking around New York and Boston, where I visited first, resembling zombies: mind-blown, freaked-out, angry or depressed that their president was being accused of such deceitful, dishonest acts, which the Watergate scandal was. Yet, here we are again; many people emotionally distraught over national politics. History repeating itself, the seesaw of life swinging back and forth, with the reliable constant of Change always front and center.

When I lived on the idyllic Caribbean island of Dominica, making monthly cargo loads of tropical fruits and vegetables shipments, I made a firm decision to divorce myself from what was happening back in my homeland, having left years before Nixon abused his powers. In effect, I did a *turtle* on myself. I peacefully withdrew to a safer place, by leaving my country for a jungle paradise where I could more easily retreat from the conflicts of my nation.

When I returned in the midst of the emotional and social uproar caused by Watergate, I experienced more of a shock than many others did over those sordid events. Not having read or listened to any Stateside news in preceding years, upon my return I went into a disorientation that felt surreal. I hadn't been prepared for the enormity of the scandalous break-in's reality. Similarly, today's events shock many, not expecting such carnivalesque antics from a U.S. President. Instead of feeling protected, though, my choosing to not keep abreast of important events regarding my Stateside countryfolk, had only kept me ignorant, not safe.

Today, I realize I had allowed myself to become thoroughly out of balance when I was an ex-pat, and refused to know what was going on back home. My anger over our Vietnam engagement had been so thorough, I'd let myself get out of touch, on purpose. But as a result of my uncomfortable re-entry back to my own country, I swore I'd never let myself get that isolated, that far removed again from America's domestic events that indeed, affect me, as an American, and as a citizen of the world.

Everything needs to be in balance. Even being *turtle-like*, detached, isolating oneself from too much bad news, too many adversities, must be balanced with knowledge of what's going on, in order for us to live comfortably in this complex world of ours. I have gotten better at balancing being informed about current affairs, even political ones. I glance at the news on my phone's app every day, but ... just briefly. I consider myself today, a bona-fide participating member of civilization's game of give and take.

Learning to balance how much or how little information is healthiest to have, and what kind of involvement a person, a spiritual activist like myself, can handle, I've discovered I am more useful having knowledge, rather than being in denial. I feel safer and more secure in the tumultuous circumstances we seem to always be in, to be more, rather than less, knowledgeable.

Sometimes we get our best lessons from our animal totems, by deciding *not to do* as they do. Again, this is a free-will situation. We get to choose which animals we think are worthy of being role models, which aren't, and ... in the case I've just mentioned, I chose to come out of my hidden-away Turtle-like shell in this phase of my life. I'm no longer the anti-this, anti-that kind of person who gets so angry I have to run away. I can measure the pros and cons, and, best of all, I have learned to exercise my free will by accepting *What is.*

Free will is how we humans are mainly different from other animals. Sure, there are stories of other animals who've exhibited astounding use of their free will, intelligence, even communication skills. For example, there's Rin Tin Tin, the German Shepherd film and TV star of the fifties, whose uncanny abilities amazed audiences, and whose cherished bloodline continues to this day. Additionally, his movie-star predecessor, Strongheart, formerly a German police-trained Shepherd, was said to have had preternatural and physical capabilities, breathtakingly written about in the slim book with the immense title, "Kinship with All Life." And, of course, every pet owner and animal *wallah* (caretaker) feels a nonverbal, intelligent bond with their charge, often preferring the silent solace and psychic comfort of them to that of their own species, other humans oftentimes thought of as conniving and evil by passionate animal lovers.

Who is to say if we humans are the only creatures upon Earth that have free will? Certainly not I. This is not a scientific study here; this is the story of my Self-discovery, and how animals have helped me along my path, either personally or by example.

What I do know is we humans have the choice, the Divine Choice, to exercise our free will at any time. And that is the greatest spiritual responsibility of all. At this crucial time, all other species need us to speak for them. Whether other species have the ability to choose freely upon their will, or they operate from instinct alone, the truth is that this planet is ruled by we two-legged, upright hominoids. We alone, for this moment in time, are the stewards of our planet.

If we stick our head in the sand about the crisis our planet's environment is in, as some extreme, politico-types tell me they're doing these days, out of either denial or outrage, stupidly ostrich-style, we will lose a lot of our life's precious, allotted energy. Because we'll need to recuperate from being too shocked over the harsh reality of the world's ways, when we're ready to get our head out of the hole in the sand, to see *What is,* really is.

Life is difficult. But it is also beautiful. We hybrid vigors are up to the challenge of leading humankind from being blinded by fear, into the Light of Love.

Drastic events can easily trigger a massive lunge into the *communal pity pot.* Which is exactly what I witnessed happening, en masse, upon my return to the U.S. during Watergate. Regardless how a certain government runs, it is transitory. Politics shift, like the wind direction. *This too shall pass,* is how the game of politics is played. When things don't work out as we want or expect them to, this is the natural ebb and flow of life. Nothing remains the same except—what we spoke of earlier—change.

So-called "bad things" have as much a purpose, as do those

deemed to be "good things."

If an individual can't accept things as they are, that person faces a challenge in which s/he has to change, mainly how they allow outside circumstances to cause them stress. Because those circumstances, as painful as they might appear to be, serve a role of being the catalyst for change. Change happens *out of necessity*, following the fashion of a swinging pendulum. Two steps forward, then some backwards, then forward, then …. This rhythm, the pattern of erratic growth, is demanded by Nature's whim. Yet, though change is natural, it causes a lot of stress for human control freaks.

When we resist change, we are not in harmony with Nature's regularly *irregular* way of progressing. Our human will must be flexible to the more powerful Divine Will, the Mystery, the Oneness consciousness that permeates the entire Universe.

Nature, another aspect of Spirit, is in control. We must come out of our Turtle-shells to observe, and marvel at how gracefully Nature dances her Change-maker moves. Joyously, we can participate in the next step of humankind's evolutionary momentum, if we let things Be as they are, instead of mourning what our own will has failed to achieve.

Turtle is slow, heavy, cumbersome, yet always moving forward. And … look what a hero he is! His ability to retreat when necessary, his fortitude, his longevity and survival skills are the stuff of legend to our human species. Look to Turtle if you feel sad, mad, or in any other way low, disheartened, or out of sorts. Go within your own Big Heart, and emulate the spiritual detachment of Turtle.

Ask then of your higher Self, as a true hybrid vigor does: "What does this uneasy feeling I have, want to show me? How can *I* change, to be more accepting of *What is*? How can I help my fellow humans become uplifted with hope from this hopeless lowness so many feel the world is now facing?"

For good reasons, we know why Turtle is considered the wisest of the animals. When things get tough, do as it does: retreat within your Big Heart. Detach from outside troubles. Go deep, dig a safe tunnel within your own heart chamber, share it with your friends and enemies in quiet dispassion. Be aware of the news, just a bit. But be strong within, and ... wait. Until the coast is clear before you stick your neck out.

◎

Turtle, at first glance, might be said by some over-achiever sorts to be "unfit to be a winner," its VW-shaped body so slow, so clunky. In fact, its contours, deemed a "disadvantage" by ultra-slim extreme types, is quite the opposite. Turtle's compact sturdiness demonstrates the inspired, but not so obvious *need* of being steady, secure, well-grounded, and efficiently patient. Turtle could be judged as a lower, less-evolved animal because its anatomical design is not considered "beautiful" like a gazelle, or "lithe" like a cheetah, neither has a bird's stunning plumage, nor a butterfly's astounding metamorphic qualities, these outer appearances seemingly superior to drab, dull Turtle's.

But if you look more closely, sharpening your perceptions by patiently observing Turtle for some minutes in its natural habitat, one is put into an almost instant state of serenity. How can one look at something so mellow, so un-stressed—so protected from outside disturbances of all sorts, predators, threats, injustices, making itself absolutely impervious to any negative input, even from Nature It-Self—without eventually realizing that what at first appears to be—lacking pizzazz or glamour—is actually the most advantageously designed torso that can withstand the most harrowing of challenges.

Let's recognize the need for this reptile's spiritual qualities to mentor us hybrid vigors, by acknowledging Turtle's majestic role in the entire animal kingdom, which of course, includes us mammalian humans. Here is a monument that does, very nicely.

In Harvard Yard, gifted to the university in Cambridge,

Massachusetts in 1936 by Chinese alumni, there is a 27-ton marble statue of a huge turtle that carries upon its sturdy back an obelisk-shaped pillar. Upon this stele is an inscription carved in Chinese characters that, to the former students, represents the role, the inspiration the mythical Turtle offers our human society.

The pillar reads, in English: "The strength of a nation depends upon the progress of civilization, which in turn is contingent upon the growth of intellectual knowledge of its people."

Folks who waste their limited life's energies being angry, disappointed, scheming for revenge instead of being grateful that the *shocks of life* are what they are—big time *change-makers*—these people will benefit from the hybrid-vigor method of copying the animals' different character traits that have been featured here.

Try to see anyone or anything you dislike or disapprove of, as *possibly* an integral, shock-provoking gift-of-awakening that has been begging to be heard by you. Keep in mind that if you feel discomfort, it means change is occurring, or … needs to occur.

People easily forget that change is not easy; its progress is filled with stages, some satisfying, some uncomfortable. Change—with all its wonderful new opportunities and expanded freedoms also has, assuredly, periods of terribleness embedded within. Whatever happens—is.

Our job as hybrid vigors is to accept *What is*. It takes practice to let go of controlling how we think things should be, and let the flow of Love take you where you are meant to be. Sometimes to the top of, and falling off of, the Waterfall of Life, the ups and down, crazies and unpredictable that push and pull us this way and that. Part of the flow of life, whether a gentle stream, a rushing river, or a treacherous waterfall we're finding ourselves within, all of it is neither good nor bad. Whatever happens is … *What is*.

If politics is your thing, cast your vote when voting is needed—we all need to vote!—then let go of the results. Leave the obsessing about how things *should be* to people whose job descriptions are focused in that area.

The Army of Love needs your clearly-directed energies for bigger and better things.

Like Turtle, we are steadfastly marching toward liberating our human condition from the fears that have kept us back from evolving, for too long now. Our time is here.

Turtle-people, one small step at a time, eyes pointed ahead; let's move forward, shall we?

CHAPTER 21

the ecstasy of love-onomics

Roostie sleeps. Yes, the awakeners get to rest, too. We watch his dreams without disturbing this hard-working messenger, so fruitfully fulfilling his duties, trumpeting his call far and wide, morning, evening, anytime the urge moves him … to shout out loud, *Wake Up!*

For now, his voice is quiet. He's nestled in a safe treetop, away from troubles, away from lurking, ever-present dangers on terra firma. Secure in knowing that his efforts, his duty, his purpose, have been fulfilled. For the present, at least, he rests.

He dreams of being able to fly, so high, so effortlessly, unlike his limited flight that only reaches upward to a low-lying branch, or a few scattered hopping wing-lifts to help him jump over logs or small streams. Unaware he's asleep, he watches himself in this dream of his. Unaware his dream is any different from what he is capable of, when awake, Roostie looks forward to having this sleep-induced pleasure each time the curtain of his chicken consciousness draws closed, enveloping him in the velvety softness of restful sleep's boundless adventure.

High in the sky of his dream state, Roostie looks down at all the troubles and dangers of his limited life here on Earth. The stalking predators, the congestion, the confusion of humans that surround him, encroaching on his feral territory, unchained as he is, totally on his own. He's a wild rooster living in the middle of my suburban neighborhood, blown in, some say, from a hurricane a couple years ago. One of my neighbors calls him after the name of that storm, Alvin. He belongs to everyone yet nobody. He's an un-tethered wild creature, belonging to himself, either awake or asleep.

Now Roostie, in a dream flight fancy, bends his neck to look at his chest and sees ... a grand and golden-breasted bird of sheening, opalescent plumage. He's become the mythical legend *It*-self, soaring high, arisen from the ashy detritus of what he once was, but is no longer.

Now a brilliant and soaring-high, emerald winged, lapis tailed and diamond-light crested-comb phoenix—he who once was our puny neighborhood Roostie (whom I spied just once, his skinny-spindly bird-legs running down our street, incapable of flying away to escape my car)—now he's flying higher than he ever thought possible! He soars upward, riding an updraft with jewel-hued wings spread wide, never having to flap because he's arrived at his dream's chosen altitude: limitless, all he's ever known, left far behind.

Roostie rockets away! Showing us, we can also.

Now it's our turn. To rise up. Unattached. Fulfilled.

Perfect and Whole.

Free at last.

Not so long ago, I came as close to dying as I've ever experienced. I've survived other near-death catastrophes; a street mugging involving a pulled gun; a close call with a hovering, very sharp knife during a robbery *in my own house* in Boston; a disgruntled lover trying to drown me; and myself once trying to convince a rascal not to murder another person in my presence, back when I was a She-pirate in the Caribbean.

This time, I came closer to checking out than ever before. Will and our two young kids were in the back of our family's SUV, sleeping, while I confidently drove through ribbons of black highway in South Carolina. Some Being watched over us, that day. It wasn't me who gripped with steel fingers the wheel of our car as it attempted to jackknife, spinning out of control after the back wheel had flown off, its bolts sheered clean, as I drove at high-speed. Some other, surely an Unseen, was on double duty that day, maybe Noname himself, preventing our entire family from perishing.

Our car wildly careening, I watched the loose rear wheel as it bounced-bounced-bounced high in the sky down the grassy median, in front of our tilted car that was fishtailing with the heavy boat we were pulling behind us. I watched with both my hands iron-gripping the steering wheel, wondering in a calm panic, *Who's in control?* Because it surely wasn't me. That heart-stopping moment stood still, everything dreamlike beyond what I could ever make up in my surreal visions.

"That wasn't me who saved us," I later told Will, after our car had been towed to safety, damaged with only a wrecked axle, leaving a hundred-yards-long groove in the highway's surface from where it dug in with the car's and boat's heavy weight.

"It had to be Noname, my angel at the wheel. I haven't got that kind of strength, to fight that death-pull force trying to flip our two-ton vessel that was flopping back and forth behind us like a fish on a hook, not a heavy boat on a two-axel trailer. I was too scared to be *that* strong. If it was *me* driving, we would have flipped! The boat was swerving and hitting cars on both sides of us, our axel digging into the road's surface only slowing us down, for God's sake! I was too freaked. I swear, Will, I just held on for dear life, watching, praying, clearly seeing what was happening, my hands clamped on, fighting the wheel, determined to not let loose my two-fisted grip, not for anything! Something else was fighting that force I felt trying to kill us, through my hands on the wheel; so I just held on best I could, praying for help, watching the drama unfold, gripping the wheel to steady it, for all I was worth. No, it wasn't me, Will."

I remember calmly glancing in the rearview mirror to see my entire family, three terrified souls in the back of our Explorer, and me up front, fighting to stop the car from flipping to our certain deaths. Noname had taken over the wheel, I knew. Sometimes it takes coming so close to dying for us to realize what we're supposed to be doing here, before it's too late.

Fate shouts ever more loudly when we don't listen to its earlier messages. Another near-fatal accident had to happen, because, remember? I'm a stubborn cookie. For a writer to be T-boned by a dump truck-sized BOOKMOBILE (so *big* and so *white*, on that gray, overcast day where everywhere I looked at the intersection— twice I looked! I swear—was a cloud-bright haze, this feat could be considered the epitome of a cosmic bad joke. That I managed to, once again, miraculously walk away from a perilous impact that totaled my *Om-mobile*, my bright red Tracker, with me getting only a minor concussion, was a billboard message if there ever was one. Later that day, when I arrived at my mother's bedside in the nursing home, after Eve had already been phoned by Will, and told about my close call, Mom spoke as matter-of-factly as if she were commenting on the outfit I was wearing.

"You could be sitting there in your spirit body, you know, Linduta," she said. "You could have left your corporeal body. But here you are."

Only then, after my mother's usual dose of well-intentioned but double-edged commentary, did I realize my not seeing the dump truck-sized Bookmobile through the haze, was nothing short of an omen. A sign of signs.

This kind of near escape makes—*should* make—a person stop. STOP! And Listen! And … feel grateful to be still breathing.

And then, after the first wave of gratitude subsides, if a person prides themselves on being consciously awake, that hybrid vigor-ish person (me) ought to assess what she plans on doing with the time she has left here to do it.

Everything is about choices, exercising our free will.

My hair felt like it was burning on my scalp, I had so much I wanted to share with the world. I need more time! There was a reason why I was allowed to walk away from that crash. My beloved Tracker was hauled to the scrapyard but my own body was unscathed, save for the bump on my noggin where it smashed into the driver's side window.

I dove into my creative work more determined than ever, assured that the sign I'd been given was for me not to waste any more time.

I remembered what Hundertwasser told me, years before:

"Pay attention to only those people who respond to your work. Forget the ones who don't. Life is too complicated. Everybody can't get everything."

Our kids were now on their own Will was healthy and involved with his own interests. I'd wasted too much time already, wrestling with those stinking inner demons, healing from Self-loathing, and helping nurture others, so many others. My angel kids, my angel husband, my pagan mama, and so many others along the way.

Thank you, Roostie. You've done a great job. I won't go back asleep again, I promise.

Noname says: "Some of us learn earlier than others, that we are not leaves being blown around by the winds of chance. Each decision we make adds up, takes us beyond what we thought we were, to who and what we are, right now.

"The more of us who choose to awaken, then learn to use our combined powers of intention collectively, for humankind's Higher Good—the sooner this world will heal. But first, heal your own Self; by far the most important choice any of us ever gets to make."

... there's always HOPE ...

CHAPTER 22

being ... one

You know already you can ask your inner Self, your own Unseen, anything, whenever you want. Just get still, let your mind clear ... then ask. And then ... listen. Try writing (or speed typing as I do) the messages down as soon as they arrive. And they will, trust me. Just keep asking, inwardly. Go all Turtle on yourself, and ask your Chief Operating Font of Wisdom, your hybrid vigor Self, your stilled-mind inner Self, ask *It* anything. When you're ready to ask, don't analyze the response you get. Just ... let it be what it is.

Learn to trust your inner connection to the Waterfall of Life. That's how we begin to trust the interconnectedness that there is with all in existence.

All of us know there is a specialness about being human. We are considered by biologists to be the *higher* primates as opposed to the *lower*, such as apes and chimpanzees. Science tells us we have a higher functionality of our brain, and researchers claim we humans use this higher evolutionary capability for greater purposes than other animals are capable of.

There is a big difference between the right and left sides of our magnificently designed human brain, one side serving very different functions than the other. We need to keep both sides in balance for an integrative, optimal human experience. However, a lot of people in today's world tend to function predominantly from their left side, the thinking, logical, analytical side of our brain; and forget to nurture, develop by using, the right side of our brain, our intuitive, creative functions. As a consequence of our digitalized era (kudos to you, reading this book!), modern people are more out of balance, more in their thinking-minds than their intuitive-side than previous iterations of humankind were when we were, ahem, a little more animalistic. The ideal, or healthiest, most wholesome human pays attention to nurturing both sides of the human brain, so their survival and creative skills can operate cooperatively, in tandem, in balance.

The left hemisphere of our brain is what keeps us feeling separate from each other. Apart. Alone. If you want to know how, see (or read the book) Jill Bolte Taylor's TED talk, "My Stroke of Insight."

Our right hemisphere allows us to experience *Be-ing in union with all that is*. Here is where we sense that Oneness. We *feel It* because we *are* all energetically interconnected, according to the brain researcher, Dr. Taylor, in her moving presentation. This sense of interconnectedness that is intuitively sensed by the brain's right side (a *sense* that some call *spiritual*), therefore, is as real as logic is, which is the left brain's particular function, of analysis. Oneness is energetic, and consciously a function of *sensing*: the right side of the brain's purpose, its role in our marvelous human, physiological makeup. The feeling of unity with all *that is*, therefore, is not in conflict with logical thinking, when both parts of our human brain's total functionality is regarded, wholesomely nurtured, and in balance. The *spiritual* sense of Oneness of our right hemisphere's functionality, you see dear reader, is just as real as the intellectual, linear thought-patterns that arise from our brain's functions of the left hemisphere.

And this is exactly what Jill Bolte Taylor experienced when she suffered a massive stroke in her thirties, ironically, as a brain researcher, to witness for herself Oneness from a purely scientific viewpoint, however startling that may seem. Thankfully, she fully recovered (she thanks her mother for that!) and the world is indeed lucky, because her scientific proof of Oneness Consciousness—the Big *It, It*-Self—*is* indisputable.

This is why, if you so choose, you are able to communicate with your Higher Self, or if you prefer, your inner angel. Your own Unseen is accessible, tangible energy within your being. A person who understands the functions of both hemispheres of the brain has no other need for proof, or any rational reason to disbelieve, that such a phenomenon as a guiding Unseen is anything less than part of our everyday human experience.

In the same manner, the ability to sense the wonder, and cherish Love in all its many scrumptious forms, is akin to Björk's wonderful over-the-top song lyrics: "I love you ... but I haven't met you yet!"

We need no proof that Life *It*-Self is magical.

When we meditate, we're nurturing the right side of our brain, making a connection to the Unseen, the Unknown, the inner Self; Love *It*-Self, just as the ineffable Force that some call God can also be called Love.

Meditate as much as you desire. How? Many people choose to practice the *art* of meditation, tuning into Oneness, by learning to turn off the incessant freight-train ruckus of the brain's noisy left side, called the logical, rational, but oh-so rude *monkey-mind*. Which, when untrained, can drown out the Stillness of our natural, unthinking mind that is directly connected to universal consciousness, aka: Love.

Learning to relax in the right side of the brain's natural state of calm Being-ness—and nothing more—is meditation.

When we watch our breath, or use any other kind of mind-stilling technique (mantra repetition, mandala- or sound- or light- or color-focusing, etc.), the left, busy side of our dual-nature brain goes into a state of rest while the right, blissful side, the part of us that feels energetically, supremely, Divinely connected to the sense of unity—with no thoughts necessary for this natural state to occur—becomes *familiarly present* in our everyday lives. One sense of reality does not predominant over the other, we are in a state of equipoise. That's when we view our everyday life as what it is—a conscious experience of Oneness.

When the two sides, our left (logical) and our right (intuitive) sides of our brain are in balance, we then effortlessly connect to the true reality that we are all One Consciousness; All in existence is interconnected. The more one visits this Oneness, which is a so-called "expanded" or "heightened" *state of mind* (but in reality, it is just the *true function* of our dually-functioning brain's role), the more one becomes comfortable with so-called higher perceptions, higher consciousness: also called the Higher Self.

Remember to *practice* meditation. It is a learned skill, like the art of conversation, or playing an instrument or acquiring any new skill that was mentioned earlier.

Our emotional and spiritual sides are just as important and need as much attention as our physical body does. If we don't exercise our birthright to experience what it's like to be a hybrid vigor, a more well-balanced *homo spiritus*, by stilling the tendencies of an incessantly thinking busy-monkey mind ... a person will feel unsettled, and (dare I say, from personal experience) plagued by neurosis. Or never knowing contentment about the way things are.

In this century's overload of too much, too much—too much information, too many choices, out-of-control chaos—now more than ever we need to purposefully balance being over-stimulated with choosing to re-charge, re-fresh, re-focus—relax. The stress of today's world is not that the world is worse, because research proves our modern world is significantly less violent than previous times in human history. But rather that we are honestly dealing with a state of *Red-Alert!* emergency, about the condition of the Earth's environment being terminally ill. We need all the foot soldiers in our Army of Love to help remedy this that we can muster, to help herald in this time—here and now—of focusing on planetary healing. Stilling a busy mind replaces the illusion that the world is falling apart—with awareness, acceptance, and most of all—hope.

Hope fosters inspired ideas of what kinds of action humankind needs to take—right away. There is no more time for debate. There are no hiding places behind phobias or fears of doomsday. We need to take action *NOW!* Holding in your consciousness the hope for soon-realizable solutions, is action enough, so please focus your mind on being positive.

Thoughts are energy. Ideas start with thought alone. If more people hold hopefulness in their thoughts, solutions will be found, and enacted, in short time.

This is fact: *Mind is the builder.*

Our race is evolving, each awakened person brings us a bit closer to all of us being *homo spiritus.*

Everything is unfolding exactly as it's meant to. There is no mistake in this precisely balanced cosmos of ours.

Crises happen to wake us up! Don't despair during times of crisis. Remain hopeful, always. This is important for all of us. It's selfish and egotistical for anyone to give up hope.

Roostie has done his job, I'm doing mine. Without having had my own personal crises, and without the world's current dilemmas, I and many others like me might still be lying out on white sandy beaches somewhere, glad somebody else is in charge of spreading Love and helping to awaken folks—so I can go back to sleep.

This environmental crisis, terrorism, the political hemorrhaging, are forms of Roostie's *Wake Up!* call. We hear the planet and its animals calling for *Help!* We see the Reveal.

Remain hopeful, nonetheless. All is well; we are now awakened.

There's need for more Roosties in the world to awaken us, to crow our hearts out! Until we're all awakened. Applaud this brave loud bird for doing such a great job. Choose to be like him. Be happy for him, too, that his dream of *trans*forming into a cloud-kissing phoenix, arising from the rubble of lesser things that he once was, is no longer just a dream, or a cherished hope—his dream *IS* his reality now.

Keep your ears open. You'll hear Roostie crowing, so buoyantly proud, so boisterously preposterous, all around us, in every imaginable setting and unlikely locale.

He reminds us to keep our own dreams alive. Dreams that we have for ourselves, our family, and for the entire world. In our hearts and minds, and through each of our actions, our dreams become our reality.

The more we activate the brain's right side, the state of non-thinking, we Be-come the great "I Am" witness of *All That Is*. Our dreams are our life's reality. Dreams await us that we could never imagine possible before.

about the author

Finding the sacred in the ordinary is the theme of teZa Lord's life and work. A student of consciousness-exploration of all types, Lord's work chronicles how she survived an irrepressibly wild youth, to paint for us her true experiences, using mystical brushstrokes and uplifting words. Her mission—as an artist who writes, and a public-speaking spiritual activist—is to clearly communicate how to achieve a more fulfilling, balanced, and holistic way of living.

Focusing on expanded awareness that is available to anyone who wishes to know inner peace, even if the outer world is terrifying and toxic, Lord's work continues to explore the evolution of human awareness and interconnectedness with all beings: past, present, and future.

Her other books are: a full-color art manifesto, *We Are ONE*; a nonfiction allegory using yoga and meditation in a true empowerment-story: *In the 'I': Easing Through Life Storms.* Listen to her calming *MindStillers* on SoundCloud and get *Army of Love* info-updates at teZaLord.com. Look for *the ZLORD Podcast*. Join @tezalord on Insta, Twitter, FB, write dearteZa@gmail.com.

teZa's motto is: *Love is the weapon of mass illumination.* She sends love and respect to each and every one of you!

CPSIA information can be obtained
at www.ICGtesting.com
Printed in the USA
FFHW010616150120
57780519-63076FF